In the Foo

In the Footsteps of Jesus

*Explorations and Reflections in
the Land of the Holy One*

Dagmar Winter

EPWORTH

British Library Cataloguing-in-Publication data

A catalogue record for this book is available
from the British Library

ISBN 0-7162-0581-5

First published in 2005
by Epworth
4 John Wesley Road
Werrington
Peterborough PE4 6ZP

Typeset by Regent Typesetting, London
Printed and bound in Great Britain by
William Clowes Ltd, Beccles, Suffolk

Contents

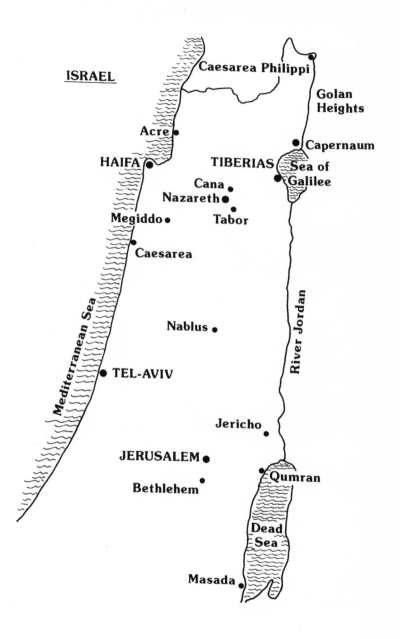

JERUSALEM OLD CITY

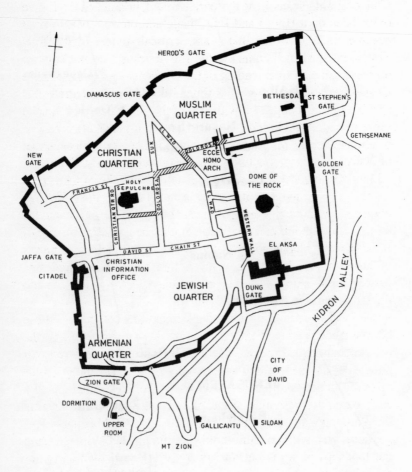

Introduction

Understanding Jesus is at the core of the Christian faith. I have twice been on a Holy Land Pilgrimage and on both occasions it became apparent to me that – as a critical student of the New Testament – when it comes to the life of Jesus I do not want to regress to an uncritical reading of the Gospel stories or to a simple Gospel harmony. At the same time, I am keen to integrate this scholarly critical approach with that of the Christian disciple who seeks to be faithful in today's world. Hence my idea of creating a pilgrimage setting for this book in which I hope to sketch an image of Jesus which is intellectually sincere as well as spiritually alive.

In this book you are invited to join a diverse group of Christians on a pilgrimage in the footsteps of Jesus. For them, it is a journey of discovery about the figure of the historical Jesus, his life and his ministry, and about their own faith. Under the gentle leadership of Julia, they are challenged to listen to the different preconceptions of Jesus they each have, and to explore new insights and new concepts. As for any of us, this process can feel deeply moving and liberating but also threatening.

The issues confronting Christians today are not merely those between believers and unbelievers or those thrown up by the developments in our world. As the Church seeks to make sense of the gospel and the world in which we live, the Christian faith finds differing understandings and expressions, often in conflict with each other. Representing some of these positions and keeping them talking with each other is one of the tasks of this book.

I hope you will find this book helpful not only in retracing the footsteps of Jesus but also in revisiting your own and your group's / fellowship's / community's steps of faith and doubt concerning the figure at the centre of the Christian faith. It would be a great joy to me if you were encouraged to visit the land of Jesus' birth yourself. Please make sure you encounter not just the holy sites but the 'living stones' too. You will be further enriched by meeting local people and by the understanding of Jesus offered by Palestinian Christians and people of other faiths.

Groups who wish to work with this book will, I hope, use the questions at the end of each chapter as appetizers for discussion but not be restricted by them. It will be important to listen for the issues each chapter raises among you in your group.

I am indebted to my friends who have encouraged me to write this little book and who have supported me hugely by offering me space and a place to write. Particular thanks are due to Rosemary Selle for invaluable help with many drafts.

I am very grateful to Gerald Burt for the initial help and guidance offered to me, then to Graham Slater and Cyril Rodd for the great care which they took over the draft manuscripts. I thank all of them and Natalie Watson for their patience with me.

DAGMAR WINTER

Notes

CE – Common Era (also known as AD)
BCE – Before the Common Era (also known as BC)

1

Setting Out

As the plane accelerated and took off, Julia smiled to herself. After she had been asked to lead a group on pilgrimage to the Holy Land, she had realized, when she knew who would be going, that she would face a challenge! The members of the party came from different churches and backgrounds and, so far as she could tell, were likely to have varied interests and strong opinions. They would find it difficult, she guessed, to believe that others could seriously hold views quite different from their own.

Her judgement was already being confirmed. During a time of prayer and reflection in the airport chapel before take-off, she had handed out pieces of paper, asking for a brief indication of each person's hopes and expectations for the pilgrimage. She discovered that Richard, who was a keen student of Scripture, was confidently hoping that the Bible stories would come alive for him in a new way. Ian, by contrast, was mainly concerned with history and wanted to understand more about first-century Palestine. Fiona, however, had little interest in the historical foundations of Christianity but was keen to see how Christians and people of other faiths lived together in the Holy Land today. Laura, Ian's wife, on the other hand, being interested in politics, wanted to learn about the environment in which Jesus lived and taught whereas Bill, for whom the death of Jesus was all-important, was eager to visit the supposed location of the crucifixion at the Church of the Holy Sepulchre. Brenda had perhaps the highest expectations: she was looking to deepen her faith by praying at holy sites. Finally, there was Brenda's husband, Harold. Harold had handed back a blank piece of paper and, smiling shyly, had said to Julia that he simply wanted Brenda to enjoy this trip of a lifetime.

As the plane crossed the Channel, there was no lack of conversation. Richard was telling Brenda how excited he was by the thought of being in Bethlehem the next day, while Fiona was warning him not to get hung up on particular places or on whether

Jesus did one thing rather than another. Ian, in turn, protested that he was certainly interested in establishing what happened and in really getting into those Jesus stories. Bill agreed with Fiona to the extent that, for him, what really mattered today was not past events but the gospel message and especially the significance of the cross. Laura added that today's places of crucifixion, where people are tortured and executed for their beliefs, should not be forgotten.

The trolley with refreshments came along the aisle, interrupting Julia's eavesdropping! She turned to her neighbour.

'How are you doing, Harold?' she asked.

'Oh, I'm fine, thanks, Julia,' said Harold. 'I'm so pleased for Brenda that we have been able to come on this trip. I just hope the others won't be arguing too much about these religious things, you know. I'm a Christian, but that doesn't mean I read the Bible every day.'

'Don't worry,' said Julia. 'I think this pilgrimage is going to have something to offer to everyone. We'll talk about that tonight.'

And they gazed out of the window as they flew over the snow-covered peaks of the Alps.

* * *

The group settled into their pilgrims' hostel in Jerusalem and, when Julia called them together after supper, they assembled eagerly and expectantly.

'Thanks for coming to this meeting,' said Julia. 'I know you're all tired from the journey but I wanted to provide a brief opportunity to gather our thoughts and set the tone for our pilgrimage. A pilgrimage is very different from a sightseeing trip. It involves us at a deep level by making us aware of our surroundings, ourselves and God – and how these three are connected.

'Let me ask you then: What's different here compared to Farnley? Just call out what comes into your head.'

'The temperature.' 'The food.' 'The plants.' 'The security checks.'

'The language.' 'The landscape.' 'The time zone.' 'The architecture.' 'The mix of faiths.' 'Our group.'

People made puzzled noises at the last contribution. Laura had called it out and Julia invited her to explain: 'Well, I think *we* are going to be different, too. We're away from our homes and our home responsibilities and our home churches, and we're together in unfamiliar surroundings.' Heads nodded.

'Thanks, Laura,' said Julia, 'and thanks to all of you. It really is very different here for us and it is good to be aware of that. We are familiar with the stories about Jesus. It is only natural that in our mind's eye we should see him walking on "England's green and pleasant land". If this means that we see Jesus as a relevant presence in our life, it has its own validity. But his life and teaching related immediately to the world of his time, and coming here can help us to understand such things better and, consequently to revise our picture of Jesus.

'Are there any questions any of you would like to ask now?'

Ian spoke up: 'I guess this really puts the cat among the pigeons, but here goes: can we really be certain that Jesus lived at all?'

Brenda looked bewildered, and Richard looked annoyed.

Julia smiled: 'A good question. And as it's a historical question, the answer must be the same as for any historical question: there is only probability, not absolute certainty. But don't be too shocked – given the evidence, it makes little sense to deny Jesus' existence as a figure in history. It is true that, around 1900, the idea was propounded that the Jesus story is a complete myth with no relation to historical reality. But such a view is based upon a number of unreasonable hypotheses; whereas the evidence pointing the other way is overwhelming.

'The case of Jesus' life is not different from that of any other historical event, including those which we read about in our school history books. And we are perfectly happy to accept as fact that Caesar lived and that the Norman Invasion took place in 1066.'

Bill and Fiona listened with growing incredulity. 'That's all very well,' Bill said, 'but what has this got to do with the core message of the gospel? We're Christian pilgrims, after all, not historians!'

Fiona added: 'I don't see why this history matters, either. It makes no difference to the beauty and truth and challenge of, say, the parables, whether they're from someone called Jesus or not.'

Bill looked at Fiona and laughed. Fiona looked at him quizzically. 'I am not laughing at you, Fiona,' Bill said. 'I'm just surprised that we seem to have a similar point of view, even if we're coming from different directions.'

'I hope this won't be the last time you surprise each other!' said Julia. 'What you are both wondering is whether historical questions really matter. I think they do. Many people believe that they know what Jesus must have been like. But the only way to assess their picture of him is to check it against the historical evidence. And the same applies to us: if we want to know the truth about Jesus, we must allow our assumptions to be challenged and reshaped by history.'

'But,' asked Ian, 'didn't you once quote someone who said that trying to discover the historical Jesus was like looking down the deep dark well of history and only seeing the reflection of your own face?'

The others laughed. 'You're quite right, Ian,' answered Julia, 'but I don't think that *not* looking down the well is an honest option. And you know, there is always the chance of seeing something of Christ even in your own face!

'Let me say just one more thing before our first day tomorrow. There are many pilgrims and tourists who are content to use this land as a giant visual aid, a sort of life-size theme park. And there are plenty of enterprising people here who offer just that, with all the commercialism that goes with it. I don't want to knock those who are desperately trying to make a living and who are so dependent on the unreliable flow of visitors. But for the sake of our own pilgrimage, I hope that we'll be able to see beyond the pre-packaged view of the famous holy sites and discover more important things.'

Harold yawned audibly – and received a dig in the ribs from Brenda! Suddenly everyone felt tired.

'When are we leaving for Bethlehem tomorrow morning?' asked Fiona.

Julia told them to be ready by 8.00 a.m., and she closed the meeting with a prayer:

Faithful God,
we thank you for bringing us together and for bringing us into
this land.
We ask your blessing on our pilgrimage:
As we walk in the steps of your Son, our Brother and Lord,
may our hearts see his face
in the Bible stories,
in the people we meet,
and in one another
so that we shall
know him more clearly,
love him more dearly
and follow him more nearly.
In his name we pray. Amen.

Questions for discussion

1. What are you hoping to get out of reading this book? (We shall come back to this at the end.)

2. In what way does the historical background matter in your understanding of Jesus?

3. What difference would it make if most of the stories about Jesus in the Gospels were made up by the Gospel writers?

2

Bethlehem

There was definitely a buzz in the group as they got onto the minibus the next morning. Already over breakfast they had exchanged their thoughts on what Bethlehem would be like. Sliding into his seat, Richard said: 'I wish I could have brought my children and especially some of their friends along.'

Bill grinned: 'Golly, I'm glad you didn't!'

'OK, I know what you mean,' replied Richard. 'But I was just thinking how many children have no idea these days what Christmas is really about. My son's friend was surprised to learn last year that we went to church at Christmas, even though it wasn't a Sunday!'

'Yes,' said Bill, 'and I'm quite sure the percentage of Christmas cards with nativity scenes is heading for zero. People just don't connect Christmas with the birth of Jesus any more.'

Brenda chipped in: 'We had some wonderful Christmas cards for sale at church. With all the lovely nativity scenes. I'm looking forward to seeing the Shepherds' Fields.'

Fiona started to sing 'O little town of Bethlehem'. The others laughed.

Laura suddenly said: 'This is all very well, starting our pilgrimage in Bethlehem. But strictly speaking, shouldn't we have started in the desert, with John the Baptist?'

Fiona added: 'Or with the annunciation, you know, when the angel came to tell Mary that she was going to have Jesus?'

'I think we would have gone to the most interesting place if we had started with John's Gospel,' said Richard with a straight face. The others looked at him blankly. Richard could be very serious about the Bible – what was he thinking of now? He went on to recite: 'In the beginning was the Word, and the Word was with God, and the Word was God.' The others were uncertain how to react. Richard was a bit disappointed. 'Just once in a while I can try and be funny too, right?!'

Bethlehem

While Bill slapped him on the back, Julia reminded them there had already been complaints that they were moving accommodation twice: from Jerusalem (for the visit to Bethlehem) to Galilee and then back to Jerusalem. So following Richard's suggestion and time-travelling to *the* beginning of everything, as in John's Gospel, would have been pushing it! 'But seriously, you are all quite right: the pre-nativity stories are very much part of the picture of Jesus painted in the Gospels. They are like pre-emptive strikes of the gospel!'

Ian looked across at his wife, Laura. Yes, as he had expected, she didn't like the use of militaristic language! But before they could pursue this, the minibus arrived at Manger Square. And there definitely was an armed presence there. Crowds of people were milling around. Richard said: 'I expect it would have been quite similar at the time of Jesus' birth: all those people from different parts of the country descending on Bethlehem to be counted for the census.' 'Yes, and soldiers among them,' added Fiona.

First they were going to visit the Church of the Nativity, which marks the place of Jesus' birth. Harold whispered to Brenda that it looked rather more splendid than the stable must have done. Together with lots of other people they entered the church and queued to see the shrine under the altar, the Star of Bethlehem. Brenda squeezed Harold's hand in excitement. People in front of them kissed the star. When it was Brenda's turn, she just looked, quiet for a moment. Beneath the star was the place where Jesus was supposed to have been born. Jesus wasn't just a figure from books and pictures and sermons and prayers. He had actually been a little baby right here. She was quite overwhelmed. Suddenly she noticed Harold giving her a little tug. 'All right, dear? I think you'll have to move on, there are people behind you.'

Next came Fiona. Fiona couldn't help feeling uneasy. She realized Brenda had been very moved, but wondered what on earth the spot as such had to do with the Christian faith today. She could not see how this star-circled hole in the ground could in any way convey the meaning of Christ's birth.

7

Richard was next. And he felt strange, too. To him, the veneration of the Star of Bethlehem bordered on idolatry. Still, it was great to be there.

Outside the church, Julia called them together, asking them to share their experiences. But no-one wanted to say much. They felt too emotional, positively or negatively. Only Ian, in his detached sort of way, said: 'I suppose no-one really knows whether this is the precise spot of the birth?'

'No,' said Julia. 'But here's a question for all of you: Why was Jesus born in Bethlehem?'

Richard said: 'Because it fulfils the prophecy of Micah. It shows that Jesus is the expected Messiah.'

Ian mused: 'I guess that's the answer you wanted, Julia. I would have simply said that Jesus was born in Bethlehem because Joseph had to go there for the census.'

'Of course you're both right,' said Julia. 'Richard's answer is the theological one. The Gospel of Matthew gives us the quotation from Micah 5: "But you, O Bethlehem of Ephrathah, who are one of the little clans of Judah, from you shall come forth for me one who is to rule in Israel." And Ian's answer is the historian's answer we find in Luke's Gospel: "In those days a decree went out from Emperor Augustus, that all the world should be registered." It's the well-known verse from the beginning of the Christmas story.

'We'll talk a bit more tonight about the accounts in Matthew's and Luke's Gospels. Let's move on now to the Shepherds' Fields.'

Brenda thumbed through her Bible. 'Do you know,' she said to Harold, 'I never noticed that the shepherds only occur in Luke's Gospel and the Wise Men only in Matthew's Gospel.'

'Is that so?' said Harold. 'Well,' said Ian, 'that's been my question all the time – I mean, how accurate are these stories really?' Brenda looked a little shocked. Fiona came to her rescue: 'I don't see that it matters at all. I think these nativity stories are more like paintings with a message than like photographs.'

Richard didn't like that: 'Oh, it's all artistic impression then? Is that what you are going to say about the virgin birth, too?'

The bus pulled up at the Shepherds' Fields, so all Fiona could respond was 'Err, yes.'

Brenda thought to herself that surely, as a Christian you had to believe in the virgin birth. It showed Jesus was special.

Clambering out of the minibus, they took in the scenery of Bethlehem, the fields, the church, the cave.

Laura sighed: 'It all looks very romantic now, but it must have been a hard life, being a shepherd here. Poor people play big parts in Jesus' Christmas story: the shepherds and Mary and Joseph with no room at the inn.'

Fiona was going to comment but then she thought she'd better keep things to herself. It had struck her how Laura's remark had some very deep truth in it. Poor people really were part of the Jesus story and they were affirmed in the Gospel. Surely that was true with or without the life of Jesus of Nazareth? She would have to think more about that.

Meanwhile they were walking across the field where the shepherds were said to have been visited by the angel with the Christmas message of peace on earth.

Laura said sadly: 'Isn't it tragic and typical that the message of peace on earth is followed by the slaughter of the innocent children?'

Ian came in on a characteristically different note: 'I don't think they really follow. As Brenda said, there are different stories in the Gospels. The shepherds are in Luke's Gospel, the slaughter of the innocent children is in Matthew's Gospel.'

Richard and Fiona both said with one voice: 'So?' Richard continued: 'That's why we have four Gospels, not every single one tells us everything.'

But Fiona said: 'I don't know why you, Richard and Ian, are so hung up on history. What does it matter? Laura said something about the *spirit* of Jesus' story.'

Richard replied: 'I believe in the Gospel stories because they are spiritually *and* historically true.'

'It's the other way round, Richard,' said Ian. 'Because you

believe in the Gospel stories, you think they *must* be spiritually and historically true.'

As a Bible-believing Christian, Richard decided there was no point in arguing with Ian. But he did want to raise the virgin birth again. Most people were interested in it, he thought, and it was perfectly obvious to him that the divinity of Jesus, the Son of God, depended on it.

Bill agreed. After all, it was not just an ordinary man who died on the cross – what would be the point of that? – but it was the Son of God, born of a virgin.

Fiona contradicted them: 'I agree that Jesus was someone special, but it is just so crude to speak of Jesus as the Son of God and claim his divinity with the virgin birth. Excuse me, but it sounds as though God mated with Mary. There must be another way of understanding "sonship", perhaps more along the lines of "chip off the old block".'

Richard shook his head, and Ian thought it was pointless to argue about these religious issues since no hard proof could be had. Listening to their argument, Brenda was fascinated but also a bit uneasy.

While all this was going on, Julia had been setting up Holy Communion for them. Now she called them together. When it came to the breaking of the bread and to the words 'We are the body of Christ', Brenda's head started spinning. Who was this Christ who had been born into this world some 2,000 years ago, yet who encompassed them all today? Well, it was her fascination with Jesus, however he was to be understood, which had brought her on this pilgrimage to the Holy Land with other Christians.

* * *

Julia addressed the group in the evening: 'We can't go into all the details of the nativity stories, so I'll just pick out three points to talk about tonight.'

1. The place of birth

Julia handed out a sheet of paper (see box): 'We so easily confuse what the two stories by Matthew and Luke tell us about Jesus' birth. There are lots of parallels but also some differences.

Matthew	Luke
1.1–17 Genealogy: Abraham to Joseph	3.23–38 Genealogy: Joseph to Adam/God
1.18–23 Angel appears to Joseph when Mary already pregnant (virgin birth introduced)	1.26–38 Angel visits Virgin Mary before her pregnancy (virgin birth introduced)
	1.39–80 Parallel story inter-woven about John the Baptist's mother and his birth
1.25 Birth of Jesus (no details)	2.1–7 Census: Nazareth → Bethlehem; birth of Jesus in a manger, no room in inn
2.1–12 Wise Men come and worship; threat of Herod	2.8–20 Shepherds come and worship
	2.21–38 Circumcision and Presentation in the Temple in Jerusalem
2.13–18 Mary, Joseph and Jesus flee to Egypt while Herod slaughters infants	
2.19–23 Return from Egypt, settling in (new?) home in Nazareth	2.39–40 Return from Jerusalem to 'their own town' of Nazareth

'These differences have always exercised the minds of scholars.
'Matthew and Luke explain the move from Bethlehem to Nazareth in very different ways. For Luke, the family home is in Nazareth and the journey to Bethlehem is just a temporary

measure due to the census. Matthew's Gospel seems to imply that Mary and Joseph lived in Bethlehem and only settled in Nazareth *after* Jesus' birth and a stay in Egypt. We are as sure as we can be that when Jesus entered public ministry, his hometown was Nazareth (cf. also John 1.46).

'Luke presents the census as the reason for Jesus' birth in Bethlehem (that was Ian's point). However, there is some uncertainty about the census because the date we assume for it does not tie in with Luke's implication that it took place under Herod the Great.

'Jesus' birth in Bethlehem has a double theological significance: it presents Jesus as the Messiah because the prophet Micah (5.1) expects the Messiah to be born in Bethlehem (that was Richard's argument) and it connects Jesus with David, since Bethlehem is the city of David. Some scholars conclude that it is unlikely that Jesus was in fact born in Bethlehem because of the different reasons given by Luke and Matthew for Bethlehem as the birthplace, the problems with Luke's historical framework, and the seeming implication in Mark and John that Jesus was born in Nazareth. The obvious theological interest in linking Jesus with Bethlehem may have led some early Christians to historicize their theological beliefs. That means that the Gospel writers' theological beliefs would have shaped the details of their nativity stories.'

Richard was aghast and others looked taken aback. 'Remember,' said Julia gently, 'we're always talking historical probabilities. There is a counter argument: the tradition placing Jesus in Bethlehem for his birth appears to be very old and there is good support in the Gospels for Jesus being of a Davidic family.'

2. The date of Jesus' birth

'It is strange to discuss the date of Jesus' birth, given that our counting of years assumes that the year 1 was the year of his birth (AD = Anno Domini = Year of the Lord). Today you will often find the abbreviation CE for Common Era (and BCE for Before the Common Era).

'Luke records that Jesus was born under Herod the Great *and* Quirinius. This is not possible historically since Herod died in 4 BCE and Quirinius became governor in 6 CE. However, Luke and Matthew agree that Jesus was born under Herod the Great, which points to the year 4 BCE at the latest. Add to this that Luke 3 indicates that Jesus was about thirty in the year 28 or 29 CE, and that unusual stellar phenomena were visible in the last years of Herod's reign, and the few years just before 4 BCE seem most likely for Jesus' time of birth.'

Ian was fascinated and would have loved to go deeper into the issues of ancient history. Brenda felt a little dismayed that matters seemed more complex than she had assumed, and that Luke could have got his details wrong. So she saw a glimmer of hope when Richard pointed out that there really was no problem with Luke's dates: Quirinius could have been involved in a census under Herod the Great before becoming governor.

Richard was pleased that Julia admitted this was a possibility, although she added that she thought it was speculative and less likely.

3. The virgin birth

'This is one of the most famous controversies surrounding the life of Jesus and you have already touched on many of the arguments. Much has been made of the quote from Isaiah 7.14 "a young woman shall be with child". This is the Hebrew version and it is only in the Greek translation that the word "virgin" replaces "young woman". However, there can be no question that Matthew and Luke describe a virgin birth, that is, a conception without human cause. For John it is not an issue and Paul does not mention the virgin birth, but then he hardly has any detail on the life of Jesus anyway.

13

'Clearly, for Matthew and Luke the virgin birth is part of their witness to Jesus Christ, to his uniqueness and his divinity. You will have to decide for yourselves:

- whether early Christian witness to Jesus might have inspired the tradition of the virgin birth in the first place; and
- whether it is absolutely necessary to believe in the virgin birth in order to uphold the divinity of Jesus.'

Richard said: 'I really find your whole approach to the Bible very difficult. You don't just accept it but question it.'

'Yes, well,' Julia responded, 'I find that biblical criticism helps us to understand more about the whys and wherefores of the way the gospel is presented in the Gospels.'

Richard looked disconcerted: 'You don't have to criticize the Bible to understand it!'

'Ah,' said Julia, 'that's a misunderstanding: in the term "biblical criticism", criticism doesn't mean the same as in everyday language where "criticizing" people often has a negative meaning. Originally, the word criticize simply means to differentiate, to distinguish. That's how it's used in biblical studies. It's true that one can analyse biblical texts to the nth degree and completely lose sight of the whole. But I do believe that God has given us critical faculties to use and that there is nothing to lose and everything to gain for our faith when we search and ask and study honestly. In fact, I think we rather lose out if we close our minds, refusing to put forward or even acknowledge our doubts and questions and just treading water.'

Richard was not convinced: 'That must depend on where those questions come from – I'm sure some of our doubts and questions can simply throw us off the track of faith.'

Brenda sympathized with that. She found the idea that Jesus might not have been born in Bethlehem very disconcerting. On the other hand, did it really have an impact on her faith? But she would hold on to the virgin birth. If anything, it helped her remember

Jesus was divine. Oh, she hoped there wouldn't be any more arguments, she didn't like that at all. And it was giving Harold a bad impression of church people.

Julia decided that this had been enough for one evening, and called the group together for a prayer:

God of strength,
we thank you for coming among us and sharing our human life
in Jesus Christ, our Brother and Lord.
Help us to deepen our understanding of one another and you
as we journey on
and give us the love that casts out all fear.
In Christ's name.
Amen.

Questions for discussion

1. What do you make of the belief that the divinity of Jesus depends on the virgin birth?

2. Try to explain what Julia's comments that 'the Gospel writers' theological beliefs . . . shaped the details of their nativity stories' means and consider whether it implies that the stories are unhistorical.

3. Brenda thought that arguments among Christians gave a bad impression of church people. How ought Christians to react when they have different beliefs about Jesus?

3

The River and the Desert

Harold woke up feeling happy. Today was to be the desert day, the one he was most looking forward to on the whole trip. As a boy Harold had loved reading stories about desert adventures and Lawrence of Arabia, and now he was going to see the Judaean wilderness. Would they see camels, he wondered? And they would be going to the Dead Sea and floating on the water. Brenda's voice brought him down to earth again. 'Harold, can you give me your empty water bottle from yesterday? I want to take back some Jordan water for little Jack's baptism. We promised.'

Ian and Laura next door were also excited. It was going to be real history today. Ian loved the thought of going to see the caves at Qumran, while Laura was interested in Masada, Herod's palace and fortress. Masada was an optional excursion and Bill was joining them on it. He had always been fascinated by the story of the Jewish freedom fighters who had held out on Masada for many months against the Roman siege, before committing mass suicide in 73 CE rather than be defeated.

In fact, thought Julia, enjoying an early breakfast in peace, there should be something for everyone on the trip today: there was the scenic ride on the coach through the Judaean wilderness, on which they would be sure to see some Bedouin. There was the stop at Jericho to look up to the Mount of Temptation. Then they would go to Bethabara by the Jordan, one of the possible sites of Jesus' baptism by John the Baptist, and renew their baptism vows. The rest of the day would be spent by the Dead Sea. Ian, Laura and Bill were going to be dropped off at Masada, while the others would enjoy a more leisurely time, floating in the Dead Sea. On their way home they would all stop at Qumran, the home of the Essene community.

The minibus driver arrived, keen to remind Julia that everyone would need to have plenty of water with them. It was going to get very hot!

An hour later they were all on the minibus and marvelling at the wilderness that unfolded before their eyes.

Julia said: 'This is how Mark's Gospel begins:

The beginning of the good news of Jesus Christ, the Son of God. As it is written in the prophet Isaiah, 'See, I am sending my messenger ahead of you, who will prepare your way; the voice of one crying out in the wilderness: "Prepare the way of the Lord, make his paths straight."'

'And then it goes on to talk about John the baptizer appearing in the wilderness.'

Brenda thought to herself that she had never realized what the wilderness looked like. It wasn't all flat as she had expected. Instead, there were countless soft hills, like folds in a big piece of cloth. They were virtually indistinguishable from each other, and she felt sure she would get lost immediately if she had to walk among them. To think that Jesus had spent 40 days and 40 nights there!

The minibus stopped in a layby. Seemingly from nowhere, Bedouin appeared with their camels and with lots of tourist items for sale. Harold was delighted! But Julia gathered the group to a vantage point from which they could see St George's Monastery clinging to the opposite side of the wadi. It was a stunning sight.

Julia explained that for geographical reasons they were visiting the first two sites that day in reverse order of the events relating to them: first, of course, Jesus had been baptized by John the Baptist in the River Jordan, then came the temptation in the wilderness.

Richard interrupted her: 'But seeing the wilderness here is also important for understanding John the Baptist and his ministry. Can't you imagine this guy appearing here in his strange clothes, saying, "Repent!"?' His dramatic gesture made them grin.

Julia suggested he read Matthew 3.1–6 to them all, the story of John the Baptist's proclamation. They listened intently; it made quite an impression as they stood in that very landscape.

17

Laura asked where John the Baptist came from. Was he part of a community, part of the Essene community at Qumran?

'We don't really know,' was Julia's answer. 'But he represents one of several Jewish renewal movements of the early twenties of the first century and he certainly got himself into trouble for criticizing King Herod's family. In fact, he paid the ultimate price for that and was beheaded – you know, that ghastly story about his head being presented to Herodias' daughter.'[1]

'I never saw him in such a political light. I thought he was just a very strict and ascetic figure, a bit dour, really, who wanted people to be, well, more dour like him,' Laura remarked.

Julia responded: 'It all hangs together, actually: John the Baptist is a conservative who's critical of the goings-on among the upper classes and in Herod's household. He sees Jewish values, culture and religion being watered down under the Gentile influence. And part of his remedy for that is a cleansing ritual: baptism, for those who want to be more than nominal Jews, for those who really want to be serious about their Jewish faith and identity. But let's just keep quiet for a moment and take in this desert landscape, where John the Baptist and Jesus came to seek clarity about their God.'

Brenda felt quite moved as they walked back. John the Baptist prepared people for Jesus by saying that there could be no half-measures with God. Jesus' call to discipleship was hardly less radical. Here in this wilderness it was all so clear. But back home, life was far more complicated . . .

After they had all piled onto the minibus again and approached the Jordan Valley at Jericho, they saw the desert wilderness give way very suddenly to lush green vegetation. They stopped in Jericho to look up to the Mount of Temptation. Bill read the story from Matthew's Gospel (Matthew 4.1–11). Some then went up the mountain in the cable car and came back enthusing about the view from the top. Fiona remarked how striking the importance of water was when you compared the green Jordan Valley with the dry desert. There was sure to be trouble in the region if people could not agree on a shared use of water. For her, conflicts like this were what temptation and evil was about, rather than having to imagine the figure of a devil or tempter.

Richard did not see it that way. In the face of the state of the world, the decay of values even within the Church, not to mention occult practices and the springing up of new religions, he found it easy to see the devil at work.

Brenda preferred not to dwell on the subject of evil. When Richard asked Julia what her theology of the devil was, Brenda was relieved to hear her say that theology was about God. Surely, it was concentrating on the will of God rather than on the devil that saw Jesus through the temptation.

They travelled on to Bethabara at the Jordan. Harold got out the water bottle and discovered that Brenda was not alone in taking some Jordan water for a family baptism. Fiona was taking some, too.

They all gathered round by the river to hear the story of Jesus' baptism, read from Matthew 3.13–17. Ian wanted to know how Jesus related to John the Baptist and pointed out that according to John's Gospel there was some overlap between their respective followers.

'Or rivalry even,' added Julia. 'Yes, it's a question we would dearly love to know more about. Some think that in his early days Jesus was himself a disciple of John the Baptist before developing his own message. Certainly there appears to be evidence in the Gospel stories that the early Christians were keen to assert Jesus' superiority over John. One way of doing this is telling the story of John's disciples leaving John in order to follow Jesus – that's the passage you referred to, Ian: John 1.35–7.'

When Ian wondered whether Jesus also baptized in his early days, Richard was certain that that was a ridiculous idea. But Ian had a surprise for him and read out John 3.22, according to which Jesus baptized at the River Jordan. Everyone looked very interested, as none of them had noticed that verse before.

Julia grinned and asked Ian to turn to John 4.2. Here it said that Jesus definitely did not baptize!

While the waters of the Jordan were lapping the riverbank, Julia summarized: 'We really can't tell for sure what Jesus' precise relationship to the Baptizer's movement was. All we can say is that there was evidently some connection and some discussion about it. And most importantly, Jesus was baptized by John the Baptist. We are all baptized, as well, baptized by the grace of God and in our living and dying we are called to follow Jesus to new life. Let's now affirm our baptismal vows.'

Like most of the group, Brenda had been baptized as a baby. She thought it was such a wonderful idea to affirm her commitment to Christ at this early stage of the pilgrimage. Following Jesus might be more of a mystery tour than she had imagined and she realized how much more there was to learn. But she felt she wanted to commit herself to this spiritual pilgrimage of her life, with the group pilgrimage to the Holy Land turning out to be such an important part of it. She wondered about Harold, though, and hoped he would feel able to take part in some spiritual way.

Harold was actually slightly taken aback and had to admit to himself that he had seen baptism simply as a church tradition rather than a literal following of Jesus' life. He had always found aspects of Jesus' personality attractive, more so than church ritual, so he found the whole idea of reflecting on Jesus' baptism and his own much more positive than he might have imagined.

Richard's baptism was only a few years ago and though he didn't like to say it, he thought his baptism as a consenting adult was far closer to Jesus' than an infant's. Feeling called by God and marking by baptism the decision to heed the call – that is what he imagined Jesus' baptism to have been like and that was how he saw his own.

So reaffirming their baptismal vows brought these very different people together and spoke to them in various ways as the closing prayer was said:

Almighty God, in our baptism you have consecrated us to be temples of your Holy Spirit:

May we nurture this gift of your indwelling Spirit with a lively faith, and worship you with upright lives; through Jesus Christ our Lord. Amen.[2]

A couple of hours later, Ian, Laura and Bill were walking around in the heat on the top of Masada, musing on the resilience and determination of first-century Jews. Was it not, they thought, a similar determination that had enabled Jews like John the Baptist and Jesus to live and die for their beliefs a few decades earlier?

Meanwhile, the others were enjoying floating in the Dead Sea. It really was just as everyone said: you simply couldn't sink. Julia watched them and suddenly felt a heavy weight of responsibility. In matters of faith, when people started to explore previously un-reflected faith, not everyone floated. Some might sink, because a sustainable faith didn't have the opportunity to develop. And all of them needed to be nurtured by the Holy Spirit.

As the minibus pulled into the car park at Qumran on their way home, some wondered whether it was worth stopping here. They had heard Richard say that Qumran wasn't even mentioned in the New Testament. However, Julia told them that the Essene Community which was thought to have lived at Qumran was part of the rich tapestry that made up Judaism around the time of Jesus.

The heat hit them as they stepped out of the minibus. After an introduction in the visitor centre, they walked around the remains of the Essenes' settlement. Julia explained that community life had begun there a good 100 years before Jesus. Qumran became famous in the twentieth century when the so-called Dead Sea Scrolls, believed to be the writings of the Essene community, were found in 1947. While featuring some Old Testament texts, the scrolls are mainly concerned with matters of the community. Its life was very strict, keeping itself separate and guarding its religious purity. With fascination Ian stared at the caves in the sandy coloured rocks where, by chance, the shepherds had found the scrolls. 'Wasn't John the Baptist one of the Essene community?' he asked.

Julia smiled. 'We've come full circle, haven't we, after starting our day in the Judaean wilderness where John the Baptist proclaimed his message. Yes, there are obvious parallels between John and the Essenes: the ascetic streak, the rites of purity. Many scholars think that John the Baptist had at least some connections to Qumran. But Judaism around that time was so multifaceted. There were many ascetic teachers around, there were other sects offering baptismal rites. And between the Essenes and John the Baptist there are obvious differences. The Essenes were a closed community whereas John addressed all the people, the Essenes had frequent washing rites whereas John's rite of baptism was a singular event in someone's life. Rather than trying to make John the Baptist into an Essene character, we should see both him and the Essenes as part of a broader picture of Jewish renewal movements of the time. And the same goes for Jesus. Just remember that during his lifetime there were many different Jewish groups and movements around.'

Slowly they made their way back to the car park. For the first time Fiona sensed something of the importance of a historical background to Jesus. It would give depth to understanding him. She put her arm around Brenda: 'This is great. Thank you, Brenda, for talking me into joining you on this pilgrimage.'

'Really?' Brenda was delighted. 'That's good. Funnily enough, I am not always so sure about this myself. I seem to know so little about Jesus and what I learn is rather unsettling.'

'I know what you mean,' Richard chipped in. He was pondering Julia's talk of Jewish renewal movements, unsure what to make of it. Then he realized that what bothered him was the way Jesus was embedded in his culture, rather than standing out as unique and striking. He would have to make sure he did not lose sight of this uniqueness.

'No meeting tonight,' announced Julia when they were back at the hostel in Jerusalem. 'It's been a long day, and tomorrow we're going on to Galilee.'

Questions for discussion

1. What does your baptism mean to you? Would it matter whether Jordan water was used?

2. What do you think of John the Baptist and what would he have to say to us today?

3. Richard wondered whether the idea that Jesus was embedded in his culture prevented him from standing out as unique and striking. Do you think Jesus is unique, and if so, in which way?

4

Galilean Beginnings

As the bus left Jerusalem, some of the group felt rather disappointed. They had not yet been able to see much of the old city at all. There was so much there waiting to be explored! But they would return – and now they were all looking forward to Galilee.

The journey took them past the West Bank cities they knew so well from the news: Ramallah, Nablus, Jenin. It was mountainous countryside, and between Nablus and Jenin Julia picked up the microphone to point out that they were travelling through Samaria. 'As you know, we are taking the most direct route to Nazareth – and given the political situation, we are very fortunate to be able to do so. When Jesus travelled in the opposite direction, from Galilee to Jerusalem, he may well have gone further east, along the Jordan.'

Bill wondered whether Jesus had wanted to remind himself of his baptism, to strengthen him on his journey. And while Brenda considered the story of the Good Samaritan from Luke's Gospel, Richard thought of John's story of Jesus meeting the Samaritan woman at the well.

Julia told them some scholars thought Jesus would have wanted to avoid Samaritan territory, because of tensions between Jews and Samaritans. 'The Samaritans were a distinct ethnic group with distinct religious features: they only accepted their own version of the Torah and no other parts of the Hebrew Bible as Holy Scripture, and for their sacrificial worship Mount Gerizim took the place of the Temple in Jerusalem. Jews at the time of Jesus felt quite ambivalent about the Samaritans and this is what we find in the Gospels, too. On the one hand, in Matthew's Gospel Jesus positively discourages his disciples to go to Samaria for their mission (Matthew 10.5), and in Luke's Gospel a Samaritan village refuses to receive Jesus (Luke 9.51–6); on the other hand individual Samaritans are praised for their virtues ('the Good

24

Samaritan' in Luke 10.29–37) and Jesus engages with them in a positive way (the Samaritan woman at the well, John 4.5–30). Interestingly, in John's Gospel Jesus' Jewish opponents think he is a Samaritan with a demon (John 8.48)!'

Brenda was listening to all of this thoughtfully. She wondered which route Jesus and his parents would have taken on that memorable occasion when the 12-year-old Jesus got left behind in the Temple, debating with the scribes, while his parents wondered where he was. As a mother, Brenda found this story very easy to relate to – the worry when children start going their own way. Then she heard Richard ask Julia about the journey of the 12-year old to the Temple in Jerusalem and back. Julia replied: 'Well, you know, different scholars think different things, but I agree with those who say that this whole story of Jesus quizzing the scribes, being so gifted at a tender age, is a legend. It's in line with other stories about famous leaders. And in line with ancient historiography – the writing of history – the story says more about the lasting significance of Jesus than what happened to him when he was 12 years old. The story also underlines the well attested custom of addressing Jesus as *rabbi* – teacher. This implies that Jesus had received some instruction and was well-versed in the Hebrew Scriptures. So I'm afraid on that basis I can't tell you which route Jesus and his parents would have walked, nor, in fact, which route Luke would have imagined them walking.'

Richard was less than happy, but he knew that this was the kind of approach Julia took. And he did have to admit to himself that she knew the Bible well, even if she came up with some pretty outrageous ideas. Brenda was dumbfounded. It was such a lovely story. Was Julia implying that the episode hadn't happened? Still, the story was in the Bible and no-one could take that away. And hadn't Julia said at a Bible study group some while ago that it was good to 'engage personally and creatively' with the Scriptures?!

Meanwhile, Harold was poring over the roadmap. 'We're almost in Galilee now,' he announced. 'Nazareth looks like quite a big place on the map.' The group looked out of the windows and could not help noticing how much greener and more fertile the country had become, the further north they had travelled. They were going to the Galilee of Jesus of Nazareth.

Julia reminded them that the Gospels frequently speak of Jesus as 'the Galilean' and asked them what they associated with this way of talking about Jesus.

There was a long pause until Brenda offered helpfully that she had always thought of Galilee as a place of rural tranquillity, an idyll, really, where Jesus lived among simple country folk and developed his thinking and teaching. Fiona added that the Galilean tag also seemed to distance Jesus somewhat from official Judaism and the Temple in Jerusalem.

'You're both right in a way. Nazareth may be a big place now,' said Julia, 'but at the time of Jesus, it was a pretty insignificant settlement. People working in agriculture lived there, and it was a backwater some distance away from the trade routes. The archaeologists think that people lived a very simple life in caves. But close by there was a thriving city – can you find it on your map, Harold, it's Sepphoris? In Herod's time, it was the capital of Galilee. It was greatly influenced by Hellenistic culture and had a big theatre. Some scholars even think that Joseph and Jesus, as craftsmen, may have found work in Sepphoris with major construction projects going on there. So while Jesus came from a rural Galilean background, he would have also known something of the urban life. And yes, Fiona, on the one hand Galilee was a fair distance away from Jerusalem, yet at the same time, with so many Gentiles around, there is an indication that Galileans were very committed to the Temple in Jerusalem, with regular pilgrimages there.'

Brenda said that Harold couldn't find Sepphoris on the map.

'Sorry, Harold,' Julia laughed. 'You're only going to find Sepphoris on a pilgrim's map, not on a current road map, since it's an antiquities park now. On today's map, the place is called Zippori or Tzipori, so spelt a bit differently. I find it interesting, by the way, that Jesus grew up in the neighbourhood of Sepphoris and is likely to have been aware of an economic and cultural world very different from that of rural Nazareth. So I think some of the parables about money and wealth may be born out of his experience of this urban–rural divide.'

Bill wondered out loud whether Jesus ever preached in Sepphoris. No-one could remember any mention of this in the Gospels and Julia confirmed that there was a great silence about Jesus going into Sepphoris or, for that matter, Tiberias. So Brenda was quite right with her assertion that Jesus was at home with country folk, although it was all rather less idyllic.

Julia was getting slightly nervous as the bus entered the sprawling town of Nazareth. So many expectations were attached to Galilee and Nazareth and it was difficult to decide where to start the visit.

Seeing the massive Church of the Annunciation, Brenda mused how it really all began here with the annunciation. Richard, on the other hand, thought of Cana as the place where Jesus did his first miracle when he turned water into wine. Laura was rather more interested in the Nazareth manifesto, as she called it, a programmatic statement of Jesus' mission from Luke 4. And Bill wondered whether they were going to visit the synagogue in Nazareth. That was the cue Julia needed. She explained that there was no certainty about the site of the synagogue. There was a Melkite (Christian) church believed to have been a synagogue on the site of an older synagogue, though nothing was definite. That, at any rate, was where they were going.

In a narrow lane beside a small building they rang the bell for the priest to open up for them.

They settled on stone benches around the walls inside the simple ancient building and Laura was thrilled when Julia asked her to read the passage from Luke 4.18–21 about Jesus standing up in the synagogue in Nazareth and reading from the scroll of Isaiah:

'The Spirit of the Lord is upon me,
because he has anointed me to bring good news to the poor.

He has sent me to proclaim release to the captives
and recovery of sight to the blind,
to let the oppressed go free,
to proclaim the year of the Lord's favour.'
And he rolled up the scroll,
gave it back to the attendant, and sat down.
The eyes of all in the synagogue were fixed on him.
Then he began to say to them,
'Today this scripture has been fulfilled in your hearing.'

After a time of silence, Fiona remarked that this was a bit like a sermon in the way Jesus spoke. First the reading, then the preaching on it.

As they talked about the passage, they realized it gave them an idea of the kind of teaching ministry Jesus would have undertaken on a regular basis. It was a true mission statement, a manifesto, as Laura had called it.

Interestingly, it also showed them that Jesus was not successful everywhere. He was certainly not successful in Nazareth, because at the end of the story, he was chased away.

But what was Jesus' basic intention? In her planning of the pilgrimage, Julia had seen this as one of the most important questions that people needed to consider. As the group sat in that simple Melkite church, they shared some of their ideas. Laura was attracted by the idea of Jesus as a liberator. 'This passage makes me proud of being a Christian,' she enthused. 'It means that as Christians we need to get involved in changing all those things which oppress people, bringing health, for example, to local communities, or campaigning for fair trade and debt relief in the wider world.'

Brenda found it much harder to warm to this particular passage. Although she could relate to Jesus helping the needy and for that reason herself did voluntary work in a charity shop, she found it difficult to respond to such social and political implications. Fiona, by contrast, was sympathetic to the Jesus of Luke 4 but wondered whether he wasn't at the same time a rather less comfortable latter-day prophet of repentance, more like John the Baptist than the Church cared to admit.

Richard's image of Jesus was different again and centred on the notion of 'power'. 'And what do you see him wanting to do with this power?' Julia asked. Richard replied without hesitation: 'Well, to convince people of the Gospel, to turn their hearts, to drive out evil forces, to transform the Church and the world, you know, "until the whole creation shall worship at his feet".'

'I find that difficult,' said Ian. 'Do you really think Jesus came to be worshipped? I mean, it sounds rather egotistical, really, doesn't it? Wasn't his purpose to tell people about God and then people discovered his whole life actually told them about God?'

Julia suggested that they revisited that issue – the question of Jesus' self-understanding, or 'messianic consciousness' – when they went to the Mount of Transfiguration.

Bill, who had been itching to comment, said that the whole Jesus story did not make sense without his passion and death. 'If you ask me what Jesus' basic intention was, I reply: his coming to save us, loving us so much that he died for us, sacrificing himself for us.'

Julia pointed out how they were all picking up different but related strands of biblical and Christian tradition. She hoped that, as the pilgrimage through the land gave rise to a pilgrimage of faith, they would identify and share many more.

At this point, the guide moved them on, leading them back out of the lane to Mary's Well, the only water supply for Nazareth, as it would have been in the days of Jesus. Many biblical stories feature special encounters at the well while drawing water, and this was the rationale for the Greek Orthodox church being built over the well. According to legend, the annunciation happened here, while Mary was drawing water.

'Whether this is the site of the annunciation or not,' said Julia, 'it seems certain that Jesus and his mother would have come to this place for water.'

The group members were given the opportunity to visit

individually the Basilica of the Annunciation, the traditional site of the annunciation for Roman Catholic Christians.

Bill set off first, and he was surprised how moved he was by the place. The smell of incense reminded him of summer holidays with his aunt. She had often taken him to Mass, and the Virgin Mary was all-sustaining for her faith – more so than Jesus, he had thought at the time. Only later did he understand more fully that Mary's importance derived from being Jesus' mother. His aunt would be thrilled at the thought of him being there.

Fiona and Laura decided to go around together. They had very mixed feelings. On the one hand, they loved all the images of Mary contributed by many different countries in the world, and it was good to spend some quiet time in the background of the Grotto while Mass was being said. On the other hand, they could not warm to the atmosphere and spirituality of the place. They were struck by the fact that here they were, on a pilgrimage in the footsteps of a man, Jesus, yet as women they did not find the emphasis on his mother especially encouraging or liberating. They decided to ask Julia later what she had to say about Jesus as a male saviour!

It was time to make their way to the bus again.

The next stop was Cana – well, one of the places claiming to be the Cana of John 2, as Julia pointed out. The Cana they visited was a little village between Nazareth and Tiberias for whose inhabitants the selling of jars and other items relating to the wedding story of Cana was clearly a major source of income. When they visited one of the churches in Cana, Julia had a surprise for them.

First she got Richard to read the story from John 2 about the wedding in Cana. When the wine runs out, Jesus turns water into wine. John's Gospel, as Julia explained, understands this to be the first 'sign' in Jesus' ministry, an indication of his glory.

Julia then invited those who were married to give thanks and pray for their marriage and those who were not married to give thanks and pray for the marriages of family members and friends. After a time of silence, she began the prayer:

We have come together in the presence of God
to give thanks for married life, our own and that of others,
to ask his forgiveness for all that has been amiss,
to rejoice together and to ask for God's blessing.
As our Lord Jesus Christ was himself a guest
at the wedding in Cana of Galilee,
so through his Spirit he is with us now . . .[1]

It was a quiet, thoughtful and moved group that got onto the bus again. Brenda squeezed Harold's hand. Richard would have loved Linda to be there.

Julia announced their last stop of the day. In the light of late afternoon they were going to make a detour to Mount Tabor, the traditional location for the transfiguration. On the way there, Julia told them that many scholars preferred Mount Hermon (further north) as the likely site. However, Mount Tabor was more easily accessible for them. 'Anyway,' she quipped, 'in Psalm 89 both Tabor and Hermon praise God's name' (Psalm 89.12).

At the bottom of the round mountain – or should it really be called a hill, Ian wondered – they clambered into taxis which took them at breathtaking pace up the serpentine road to the top. Once there, they enjoyed a beautiful view of the entire region. The Franciscan Church of the Transfiguration was on the summit, but it was such a beautiful afternoon that Julia got the group to form a circle in the open while Ian read the account of the transfiguration from Mark 9.

Standing there together, they all felt what a powerful story this was. Ian noted how in Mark's Gospel the story followed Jesus' first foretelling of his suffering, death and resurrection. Brenda remembered how Julia had said they would talk about Jesus' self-understanding on Mount Tabor. 'The transfiguration', she reflected, 'must have been such an encouragement to him!'

Julia called this a psychological way of looking at the story. Yes, it was an encouragement, but primarily for the hearers and readers

31

of the Gospel story. They were encouraged to hear Jesus' divinity affirmed in his life of lowliness and suffering. Like the baptism story, the transfiguration story backdated elements of the risen Christ into the life of the earthly Jesus. Some scholars called the transfiguration story a misplaced Easter story! It was nineteenth-century theology with its predilection for the psychology of the individual which read a particular self-understanding or messianic consciousness into Gospel stories.

Richard was annoyed. Why, why, why did Julia confuse Brenda and deny the truth of the story? If Jesus could rise from the dead, why shouldn't there be a transfiguration experience on the mountain before his death?

Ian had been interested in Julia's remarks but didn't want another argument about these matters. Having been the one who read the story, he was particularly interested in the people on that mountain top: Peter, James and John, and then, of course, Moses and Elijah.

Laura just loved the symbolism of Jesus in continuity with the great heroes of the Jewish faith, Moses and Elijah standing for the Law and the Prophets. 'In continuity, yes, but also superseding,' added Richard.

And the three favoured disciples? Julia had to explain that it wasn't for another couple of days that they would be thinking about the calling of the disciples. Clearly, their pilgrimage was not quite following a chronological approach here. But Peter, James and John could be seen both as particularly close to Jesus during his lifetime and as guarantors of the Jesus tradition in the early Church. They were also present in Gethsemane.

Fiona thought that his friendships added a very human dimension to Jesus – while he was loving to so many people he met, he also had people he was particularly close to.

Julia grinned: 'I wish you could say that to some people in our congregations who think the minister doesn't need friends! Let's go and have a look inside the church. You'll notice it has three storeys and tries to tell the story of the transfiguration through its architecture. In 20 minutes we'll meet at the taxi and travel down again.'

Once back down, pleased to have arrived in one piece, they were all ready to let the bus take them to the hotel in Tiberias where they were to stay for the next few days.

* * *

Following a lovely meal, they gathered in the hotel lounge to share some reflections on the day.

Brenda said: 'When I think of all I've seen and heard over the last days, it feels like a big tangled heap right now. There is so much, but I'm not even sure where it begins. Where does the Jesus story start: with the annunciation, with his birth, with his baptism, with his sermon in the synagogue in Nazareth or with the first sign in Cana?'

Julia started to talk about Galilee: 'Today we have had our first day in Galilee. While arguably the most important part of Jesus' life took place in Jerusalem, most of the Jesus stories are located right here.

'So what is Galilee at the time of Jesus? It's a region in Palestine, governed by King Herod the Great (37–4 BCE) and his son Herod Antipas (4 BCE–39 CE). The establishment of new Hellenistic cities like Sepphoris and Tiberias around the time of Jesus' birth meant that there was a strong urban element in Galilee, living cheek by jowl with a poorer rural population. The cities also accounted for a higher proportion of non-Jewish people in Galilee. Both the rural–urban and the religious–ethnic divide had crisis potential.

'This was the environment of Jesus the Galilean, and each Gospel writer highlights particular aspects of the Galilean beginnings.

'For John's Gospel, the beginning of Jesus' ministry is the first step of his self-revelation, demonstrated by his turning water into wine at a wedding feast. But before that, John also has the prologue about the Word becoming flesh, John's Christmas story, which starts off the Jesus story.

'For Luke, who wrote the Gospel as well as Acts, the annunciation together with the Christmas story forms part of and prepares the initial stage of salvation history. This takes us from Galilee to Jerusalem before going on, in Acts, to Rome. The marker is set out with the passage from Luke 4 that we listened to in the Melkite church.

'And finally, all the Gospels have very high regard for the baptism of Jesus, which may or may not have taken place in Galilee. Yesterday, we visited Bethabara, but another possible site of Jesus' baptism is further north from here, at Banyas, near the source of the Jordan.

'Where does the Jesus story begin?

'You can answer that question on various levels.

'Doctrinally, you may well want to start with the story of the incarnation, whether with Luke's or Matthew's narratives or with John's more abstract presentation.

'As far as the life of Jesus is concerned, his baptism by and his association with John the Baptist, whatever their precise relationship, is clearly a key event at the beginning of his ministry. The expression of divine sonship is, I would say, a later interpretation of the event, but Jesus' public ministry seems to have begun after this.

'The Nazareth manifesto was not announced, even according to Luke's Gospel, right at the very beginning of this public ministry. But it was another key event because Jesus is "coming out" in his home village and experiences a rejection that was a sign of things to come. If you want to speak of Jesus' growing self-understanding, I would pin it to events such as these, when he began to realize that what he had to say was not universally accepted and that, if he carried on with his teaching and ministry, he would get into very serious trouble. Perhaps it is better to speak of a growing sense of vocation rather than self-understanding or messianic consciousness.

'Tomorrow, we shall need to look at how this vocation related to his Jewish faith and contemporaries.

'Let us end this evening and this day with a prayer. Here's a verse from a well-loved hymn:'

O Sabbath rest by Galilee!
O calm of hills above,
where Jesus knelt to share with thee
the silence of eternity,
interpreted by love![2]

Lord Jesus Christ,
as we discover the places where you grew up, lived and worked,
we ask you to deepen our understanding of your life and
ministry here in Galilee,
so that the love which permeated your life may grow in us.
Amen.

Questions for discussion

1. What do you think was the main message and intention of Jesus?

2. Read the story of the transfiguration in Mark 9. How would you interpret it?

3. Where do you think the story of Jesus begins? What difference does your decision make to understanding him and his work?

5

Home in Capernaum

Julia had decided that the fourth day should be a more restful one. It was important that the group should get a feel for the place, enjoy the Sea of Galilee and let impressions sink in. The place they were going to visit was actually one of Julia's favourite Galilean sites, the ruins of the synagogue in Capernaum. During the ten-mile drive from Tiberias, along the lakeside, she would read with the group a few of the Jesus stories associated with Capernaum.

As the minibus pulled away from the hotel, Laura was particularly looking forward to the day. She knew where they were going and she had said to Richard that she thought it was really important to visualize Jesus in his Jewish setting, teaching in the synagogue, arguing with his Jewish friends.

Julia showed them a map of ancient Palestine and pointed out that Capernaum had been on the border of the region governed by Herod Antipas. Hence the tax booths and the tax collectors with whom Jesus ate and out of whose number he called Matthew. Capernaum was Jesus' hometown where he taught and healed many. It was also home to a small garrison with a centurion.

Harold, looking over the map, pointed out that the Hebrew name of the place was Kfar Nahum. Brenda had already spotted that on the road sign. 'But wasn't Nazareth Jesus' hometown?' she enquired.

Julia said that Nazareth was clearly the place where he was brought up, but during the time of his public ministry, he appeared to be most closely associated with Capernaum and based there. Mark has the first healing and teaching story located in Capernaum (Mark 1.21–8) and, after some travels around Galilee, Capernaum is referred to as Jesus' hometown (Mark 2.1; Matthew 9.1). 'It is certainly described to us as the hometown of Simon Peter, whose house was there. In fact, you will see the remains of a house which is assumed to be that of Peter not far from the synagogue. And the synagogue is where we shall go first.'

Bright sunlight shone on the white limestone walls of the ruins of the synagogue at Capernaum. Laura was quite overawed – to think that this was the very synagogue where Jesus had taught! Sadly, Julia had to disappoint her. She explained that the remains of the white synagogue, now partly reconstructed, belonged to a later building, probably from the late fourth century. But this had been built on top of an older, basalt synagogue, some parts of which were visible and exhibited in the grounds. This would have been the synagogue well-known to Jesus. It had been destroyed by the Romans in 69 CE during the First Jewish War.

The group assembled in the area which would have been the central prayer hall of the later synagogue. At the time of Jesus, the Jewish community in Capernaum is thought to have been too poor to build a synagogue. Julia read them a verse from the well-known story in which some Jewish elders asked Jesus to help the centurion. They said, 'He is worthy of having you do this for him, for he loves our people, and it is he who built our synagogue for us' (Luke 7.4–5).

Then Bill read the passage from Mark's Gospel (Mark 1.21–8) according to which Jesus and his disciples went to Capernaum, where Jesus entered the synagogue on the sabbath and taught. The story ends with an exorcism taking place on the sabbath. Julia then asked Harold to read the story a little further on (Mark 3.1–6), in which a man with a withered hand is healed in the synagogue on the sabbath. This results in the Pharisees and the Herodians plotting Jesus' death.

Laura asked whether this episode reflected the later view of Christians who had turned against the Jewish people.

Julia agreed that Mark had carefully structured his Gospel and led his readers to expect the passion story from the outset. So the introduction of Jewish hostility to Jesus here was a literary device rather than a historical report.

Wanting to pursue the matter further, Laura pointed out that there was a definite problem with anti-Judaism in the Christian faith which needed addressing at its root. Here they were, on the site of a synagogue where Jesus had taught. Was his Jewishness taken seriously enough?

Richard surprised them by saying that he thought that this was one of the key questions for him: how Jesus' Jewishness could be respected while still holding fast to his uniqueness.

When Harold mumbled that every person in this world was unique, anyway, Julia asked them to think about what it meant to them that Jesus was a Jew.

As they walked around the site exhibits, Fiona was particularly taken with a depiction of the Ark of God on wheels: it was a very vivid sign to her of God's companionship on the journey of life. Suddenly Laura nudged her. She was very concerned to find a swastika in stone and asked the local guide about it. It turned out to be an innocent geometrical design of the time. Richard sidled up to them and told Laura that he appreciated her concern for the Jewishness of Jesus. But if Jesus did not in some way stand out from his Jewish contemporaries, neither his death nor his importance for Christians later made any sense. Laura shrugged; she was concerned precisely with the way Judaism was depicted in order to make Jesus stand out ever more clearly and brightly.

In the end, Brenda summed up the problem they had: they weren't really sure what it meant that Jesus was a Jew.

Julia had heard what they were saying and called them together. 'Let's look at what we know of Jesus that can make it hard for us to understand.

'On the one hand, he clearly followed Jewish faith and custom, taught in the synagogue and celebrated festivals: "He went to the synagogue on the sabbath day, as was his custom." On the other hand, he claimed the authority to reassess some of the current laws and customs by appealing to the created order: "The sabbath was created for people, not people for the sabbath." On the one hand, he relaxed laws like the sabbath law; on the other hand, he intensified the requirements of the law – see, for example, his teaching on anger or adultery in Matthew 5, when just thinking or saying something is counted as bad as the actual deed. On the one hand, he argued from within the Torah, on the other hand, he said, "You have heard . . . but I say to you . . .". On the one hand, he saw his mission as exclusively to his fellow Jews, on the other hand, by weakening the sabbath commandment, he threatened a crucial identity marker for the Jewish people. On the one hand, he said to the scribe, "You are not far from the kingdom of God," on the other hand, he was in sharp conflict with some of his Jewish contemporaries.

'In all this teaching you hear a definitely Jewish voice which is at the same time quite distinct.

'Tonight I'll give you a brief overview of the various Jewish groups at the time of Jesus and we'll have a look how he fits into that. But now, let's walk across to Peter's house.'

They peered with interest at the remains of what was thought to have been part of Peter's house. A church had been built over it, enabling visitors to look at the remains from above. Ian was incredulous: 'How can they know that this was Peter's house?' Julia replied that it was not certain at all, but at least it gave people an idea what a house of a fishing family at the time looked like. And she promised that they would be looking at the calling of the fishermen-disciples the following day.

Just as they were about to leave the site, Richard said he had another verse of Scripture appropriate for the place.

'Woe to you, Chorazin! Woe to you, Bethsaida! . . . And you, Capernaum, will you be exalted to heaven? No, you will be brought down to Hades. For if the deeds of power done in you had been done in Sodom, it would have remained until this day.' (Matthew 11.21, 23)

Uneasy laughter broke out.

Julia said she could not help adding to that that there was actually evidence of a strong Jewish Christian community in Capernaum in the second century. Matthew 11.23 was probably not their favourite verse of the New Testament!

As the minibus took them back, they stopped at the foot of Mount Arbel and some of the more energetic climbed the mountain to get a splendid view of the lake. The others enjoyed the lakeside by the hotel.

* * *

In the evening, as promised, Julia gave a brief outline of the Jewish groups in Jesus' time.

Scribes

A 'scribe' is literally someone who can write a text. In the more specific context of Judaism the word describes someone who is versed in the Hebrew Scriptures.

No other sources but the synoptic Gospels suggest that scribes are a specific unified group. At the same time, the Gospels differentiate between scribes: some friendly, others hostile; some from Jerusalem, others from Galilee. In a sense, Jesus himself is a scribe since he is a religious teacher.

There is an overlap between scribes and Pharisees (some are both scribes and Pharisees). Jesus appears to have had ambivalent relationships with both.

Pharisees

The Pharisees had originally been a political party but became a religious movement concerned with making piety liveable for people. In that sense, by helping ordinary people to come to grips with their religion, they overlapped with Jesus. Luke records an incident where friendly Pharisees warn Jesus of Herod Antipas (Luke 13.31). Although there are so many negative comments about the Pharisees in the Gospels, this is probably a sign of Jesus' closeness to them. They occupied common ground and had issues to argue about. It appears that Jesus' main objection to the Pharisees concerned their defensive inclination to keep themselves separate and pure and to avoid any danger of becoming defiled. (The word 'Pharisees' means the 'separate ones'.) Jesus turned their thinking on its head when he demonstrated how purity rather than impurity was infectious.

Sadducees

The Sadducees are probably best known to us for their rejection of belief in resurrection, a matter in which they disagreed with the Pharisees. But they also represented a different class and different interest group within the Judaism of Jesus' day. They were the Temple aristocracy, often with little time for the concerns, rules and regulations of the Pharisees but greatly concerned with their own power and influence. Hence Jesus' authoritative cleansing of the Temple did not go down well with them.

As members of a ruling class, they were also open to criticism for collaborating with the Roman occupying forces. We get the distinct impression that Jesus had much less to do with them than with the Pharisees.

Zealots

It has been thought that 'the zealots' were a unified group of resistance fighters who were chiefly responsible for the revolt of the Jewish War 66–70 CE. More recent scholarship understands the term 'zealots' much more as the name for a loose coalition of various groups opposing Rome. The motivation of these groups would have thus stretched from strictly religious and ideological to criminal.

One of Jesus' disciples, Simon, is called 'the Zealot'. Given that this appears to be a distinguishing title, it indicates that no other disciple was particularly associated with the zealots. We have no other evidence of Jesus relating to zealots.

Julia ended the evening with a prayer.
　'Let us pray.'

Lord our God,
We thank you for the community of faith in which Jesus grew up
and learnt to believe.
We give thanks for the Jewish people through the centuries and
pray that you will guide them through these present days.
Enlighten also our hearts to seek to worship Jesus not by
denigrating his Jewish brothers and sisters but by discovering
the riches of his Jewish heritage of faith.
We pray for dialogue between Christians and Jews
and that good fruit for all people may grow out of this.
In the name of Christ who loved his people we pray.
Amen.

Questions for discussion

1. What does it mean to you that Jesus was a first-century Jew, and does that have any bearing on the way Christians should relate to Jews today?

2. Are there parallels to Jewish law in Christianity, and if so, how should a faithful disciple of Jesus relate to them?

3. Jesus drove out an evil spirit and miraculously healed the man with a withered arm. How would you explain this to an agnostic friend?

6

The Sea of Galilee

Bill woke up with the feeling that there was something amiss. Suddenly he remembered: they were going to cross the Sea of Galilee by boat. Much as he liked sailing, his sea legs were not what they should be and he always worried about these things.

His fears were somewhat allayed when they looked out over the lake at breakfast. It really was as flat as a millpond. 'Did you hear the boat out on the lake last night?' asked Richard. Laura and Fiona groaned. The sounds and beats of the disco boat had been unmistakable as they had tried to sleep! Evidently, the Sea of Galilee offered varied attractions . . .

Then Harold pointed out a wooden boat approaching on the lake: 'It looks kind of old-fashioned! Is this the one we're going on, Julia?' Julia nodded. This was the so-called Jesus Boat, modelled on an archaeological find thought to originate from the time of Jesus. Bill looked slightly worried and Laura had to laugh: 'Really, Bill, it'll be quite all right. And it's such a lovely day. The worst thing that can happen is that you'll get sunburnt!'

An hour later, the happy band of pilgrims set sail from Tiberias, sharing the boat with another group. There was a mast for a sail, but the boat was engine-powered. After ten minutes or so, the crew switched off the engine. It was quite still.

One of the crew donned a white toga-like garment and picked up a net conveniently stored at the back of the boat. He was about to demonstrate how the fishermen would have fished in Jesus' time. With a dramatic swing of the arm (and to the clicks of many a camera), he cast the net into the lake.

Someone from the other group read Mark 1.16–20, the calling of the fishermen Simon and Andrew and of the sons of Zebedee, James and John. They all left their nets and followed Jesus.

Quietly, Brenda began to intone one of her favourite hymns:[1]

Jesus calls us! O'er the tumult
of our life's wild restless sea.
Day by day his sweet voice soundeth,
saying, 'Christian, follow me!'

As of old Saint Andrew heard it
by the Galilean lake,
turned from home and toil and kindred,
leaving all for his dear sake.

Julia asked Bill to read another lake story, the stilling of the storm, from Mark 4.35–41. Here Jesus is asleep in the boat with his disciples when a storm begins to batter the boat. Panick-stricken, the disciples call on Jesus, and after stilling the wind and the sea, he chides them for their lack of faith.

While they listened to these stories the boat moved gently, tiny waves lapping against the bow.

Julia quietly prayed with them the collect for St Andrew's Day:[2]

Almighty God,
who gave such grace to your apostle Saint Andrew
that he readily obeyed the call of your Son Jesus Christ
and brought his brother with him:
call us by your holy word,
and give us grace to follow you without delay
and to tell the good news of your kingdom;
through Jesus Christ our Lord. Amen.

To everyone's surprise, Fiona put into words what several of them felt: 'Of course I could understand these stories back home and I could imagine a boat. But it does make a difference hearing it all in this setting, with a view of the Galilean hills around.'

The engine was started up again and they continued their journey across the lake. Julia pointed out Capernaum, and the Mount of Beatitudes and Tabgha, where they were going the next day. It was

44

indeed different, seeing these places from a fisherman's perspective, as Richard put it.

Ian sat down next to Julia and said: 'Tell me, Julia, did they really live like that? I'm thinking of those first disciples, Andrew and Peter and all the others. According to the stories in the New Testament, Jesus called them and they just dropped everything and followed Jesus around. Is that what Jesus wanted and expected? Because if it is, I reckon the Church is in trouble!'

Harold joined in: 'Yes, our son once had ideas like that. He wanted to join a group who went around preaching. Pretty idealistic he was, and he would have been penniless in no time! I think he was simply afraid of the responsibilities and discipline you need to hold down a regular job.'

Julia smiled: 'Yes, the story we heard about the calling of the first disciples does show us Jesus asking people to leave everything else behind. And the story has been used to justify irresponsible behaviour.

'But the calling of the fishermen is a carefully crafted scene. Mark wanted to emphasize that faith is no hobby, and coming to faith involves accepting the authoritative call of Jesus. I think that's important and I'd like to hold on to it. The Gospel writers have different emphases, though, on how disciples are called. While Mark has this direct call, John's Gospel stresses the importance of third persons who bring someone to Jesus, like Andrew bringing Simon Peter and Philip bringing Nathaniel. Did you notice that the collect for St Andrew's Day doesn't actually refer to Andrew's calling as we read it in Mark's Gospel but is taken from John? "He brought his brother with him" – you'll only find that in John's Gospel.

'Matthew and Luke, on the other hand, show us how Jesus dampens people's enthusiasm. When people announce to Jesus that they want to follow him, he warns them to consider the consequences: If you look back, you cannot be my disciple.

'But all this is just one kind of discipleship and friendship with Jesus. Of course, there are the radical followers who are itinerant preachers. But there are others: those Jesus shares a meal with, and those such as sinners and tax collectors who welcome him into their homes; and there are those, especially women, who serve and support him wherever he or they happen to be. None of these seem to be expected to leave everything and literally follow Jesus around.'

Brenda was very moved by this: 'You know, I never heard it presented to me like that. I always felt ultimately second- or third-rate as a disciple of Jesus. I thought that if I really wanted to be a proper Christian, I would have to live as I know I can't. I couldn't give up my family. I never thought there were these different ways of being a disciple in the New Testament.'

'Yes,' Ian added, 'and different ways of being called, too. It doesn't have to be the sudden conversion!'

The boat was nearing Ein Gev, where they were going ashore. Lunch awaited them, and St Peter's Fish was the dish of the day. As they enjoyed their meal together, some shared the stories of how they had become Christians. Other people had been instrumental in every case. For Brenda the influence of the family had been essential, for Richard it had been a close friend and colleague, and for Laura a group of Christians campaigning on justice issues.

Bill was pleased to be on dry land again and never more so than when he looked up and noticed that the weather had changed dramatically. Clouds and a strong wind had come up, and the lake which had been so calm only half an hour ago had angry waves dashing against the shoreline. 'Look at this,' he said. 'I'm glad we're not out there now. This really looks biblical!'

Julia was rather taken with this unplanned example of a sudden change of weather on the Lake. Bill, who had read the story of the stilling of the storm, felt that the disciples being rocked about in their little boat were a pretty good image of the current state of the Church.

Ian agreed with him, but argued that the story itself hardly had the Church in mind. For good measure, he added: 'And neither did Jesus have the Church in mind!'

'Why then do you think Jesus chose twelve disciples and gathered people around him – and commanded them to teach others?' This was Richard's critical question.

Ian turned to Julia to ask whether the story of the stilling of the storm was about the Church.

Julia thought that the Gospel writers understood it like that. They were, after all, addressing the situation of the Christian communities they were part of. 'But what did Jesus himself mean? You couldn't really call Jesus' twelve disciples the core of a church, could you?' Ian insisted.

'Well, yes and no,' said Julia. 'Jesus was a teacher and he taught his disciples the chief task of preaching the kingdom of God. I guess that's still the task of the Church today.'

'And to preach Jesus as the king of this kingdom!' added Richard.

'Yes, Jesus has become part of the message of the kingdom, and we see that happening in the New Testament. It's been called "the proclaimer becoming the proclaimed". But this happened in a time span that Jesus did not anticipate. Really, Jesus expected the coming of the kingdom as a great and overwhelming event in the lifetime of some of his disciples. So he certainly didn't envisage the Church.'

Richard was not at all convinced: 'What about all those passages where Jesus talks about issues in Christian communities? Are you saying these were all made up by the Gospel writers? The command to teach and baptize, the instructions about how to deal with conflict in the Church? And what about Jesus calling Peter the rock on which he will build his Church?' (Matthew 16.18).

Julia did not think that all this had been made up by the Gospel writers. Rather, she said, they wrote from within the situation in their communities and surrounded by the presence of Jesus in two ways: the presence of Jesus in the stories they were passing on and the presence of Jesus in the living Christ they knew and worshipped. Anticipating their post-Easter role, in some passages in the Gospels the twelve were called 'apostles' – in other words the ones who were sent out.

47

Ian wanted to get back to the twelve disciples Jesus had called. Wasn't there something symbolic about that number, he wondered?

Laura was quick to answer. 'Calling twelve disciples stands for Jesus wanting to bring together the twelve tribes of Israel, to rejuvenate and reform the Jewish people in the face of the coming kingdom. And that's something we need to bear in mind in our Christian attitude towards Judaism.'

Julia nodded. She reminded them of the verse in which the Twelve are promised that they will sit on the twelve thrones and judge the twelve tribes of Israel (Matthew 19.28).

Ian wondered whether the throne of Peter wouldn't be a bit higher than the others! Julia laughed: 'Oh, don't remind me of all those silly jokes about Peter and his role as gatekeeper of heaven! The answer is that his throne is probably no higher than the others, but it's good to remember that like any human being Jesus had a circle of friends he was particularly close to, namely Peter, James and John. Those three share both the transfiguration and the scene in Gethsemane with him.'

This appealed to Brenda. She thought of her best friends and what she had shared with them. But wasn't there the special disciple, the one that Jesus loved? She had always found this a difficult one. On the one hand, it was understandable the Jesus might have had a very best friend and confidante, on the other hand 'the special disciple' smacked of favouritism that was not easy to reconcile with Jesus' love for all people. When Julia showed her some of the New Testament passages where the beloved disciple is mentioned, it turned out they were all in John's Gospel. Julia explained that this disciple was thought to be close to John's community. He was their authority. His special role in John's Gospel, alongside Peter, was probably rather more a reflection of the beloved disciple's importance to the Johannine community than to Jesus.

Back at the hotel that evening, they talked further about their discipleship and the Church today. For Laura, it was important that the Church not only preached God's kingdom but also provided the space where the values of God's kingdom and its people could flourish. So Jesus would be present there in a meaningful way.

'I still love that image of Jesus sleeping in the boat when it's tossed around by the waves,' said Bill. 'The big church institutions we have today may be more like ocean liners, but when it comes to the real basic stuff of the kingdom and our involvement as disciples, aren't we all back in that little boat?' – 'And looking a bit green?!' Ian teased.

Julia said she always felt a tension when thinking about discipleship. On the one hand, it was important not to forget the radical commitment it called for, and that could mean resisting the more comfortable instincts of the Church.

On the other hand, it was important to discover appropriate forms of discipleship for people in their life situations. The New Testament showed there were more disciples than the Twelve and there were different ways of being a disciple. What they had in common was that, in the literal sense of discipleship, they were learners. And none more than Peter showed that human discipleship, like any learning process, includes its fair share of errors.

The day closed with a prayer:

Gracious God,
we thank you that you have called us to follow your Son Jesus Christ.
Give us grace and courage to learn and grow in our discipleship that we may become people of your kingdom,
now and in the age to come.
Amen.

Questions for discussion

1. What does discipleship mean to you?

2. By interpreting the boat as a symbol for the Church, Julia could be accused of evading the problem of Jesus performing a miracle by quelling the storm. How do you understand the story?

3. Julia said that Jesus did not envisage the Church because he expected the kingdom of God to come in the lifetime of some of his disciples. What has happened to the kingdom of God, or was Jesus wrong?

7

The Mount of Beatitudes and Tabgha

Fiona felt happy as she walked uphill. The lack of exercise on the trip so far had bothered her and she was glad to be striding out. And while she firmly reminded herself that there was nothing special for her about the mountain as such, she did appreciate its association with Jesus' beatitudes.

From the church on the slopes of the so-called Mount of Beatitudes there was a wonderful view of Lake Galilee. Small wonder, thought Fiona, that generations of Christians had pictured Jesus teaching the crowds here. As she had expected, Julia got one of them to read from Matthew's Gospel, chapter 5: 'Blessed are the poor in spirit, for theirs is the kingdom of heaven. . . .'

'What about Luke's beatitudes?' asked Laura. She was thinking of 'Blessed are you who are poor, for yours is the kingdom of God' (Luke 6.20). 'Since we did a Bible study a few years ago and compared Matthew and Luke, I always think of Luke as so much clearer, more direct. I feel Luke is closer to what Jesus might have said.'

Brenda looked puzzled. 'Is there really such a difference? Haven't Matthew and Luke just put the same thoughts differently?'

Laura was sure that it was quite different. After all, Luke didn't have a Sermon on the Mount but a Sermon on the Plain. And as far as she was concerned, his beatitudes really were much more plain-speaking!

Everyone looked at Julia, expecting her to respond. She got them to look up the parallel passages from Matthew and Luke.

Matthew 5.3–4, 6:
Blessed are the poor in spirit, for theirs is the kingdom of heaven.
Blessed are those who mourn, for they will be comforted.
Blessed are those who hunger and thirst for righteousness, for they will be filled.

Luke 6.20–2:
Blessed are you who are poor, for yours is the kingdom of God.
Blessed are you who are hungry now, for you will be filled.
Blessed are you who weep now, for you will laugh.

Apart from Laura, they were all quite surprised at the differences.

Julia asked them which beatitudes they encountered in their life and worship. Brenda said that the one from Matthew for those in mourning was often used at the beginning of a funeral service. Harold thought it would sound a bit harsh to give mourners Luke's version, saying that the weepers would laugh!

A beatitude from later on in Matthew's list was Laura's favourite introduction to the 'Peace' in a service, 'Blessed are the peace-makers, for they will be called children of God.' As they looked across the lake to the Golan Heights, scene of so much fighting in the past, she expressed what they all thought: 'It's an idyllic place to think of Jesus saying these beautiful things, words of peace and all that. But what do they mean in a world of such bitter and entrenched conflict?'

Bill pointed out that the beatitudes were also used in penitential prayers. They were then like a mirror held up in front of people, to show how far we all fall short of the ideal.

'I've had my fair share of Christians telling me I'm not good enough,' Fiona protested. 'I can't imagine this is what Jesus wants us to take from the beatitudes!'

Brenda, meanwhile, was just sitting under a tree and gazing out to the Lake. Why people had to argue like this was beyond her. What mattered was that Jesus blessed people who were unlikely to be called blessed. It held out such hope.

When the group moved on, however, it was not Brenda but Richard who was suddenly missing. He had gone down to the lake again and was skimming flat pebbles across the water. Richard struggled with the beatitudes. They were such an important part of Jesus' preaching, but they did not seem to have at their centre what Richard saw as the core of the gospel: faith in Jesus. It was all too easy to treat these words of Jesus simply as part of a general human aspiration, a political programme even. That was how Laura saw it, and Julia would not contradict her outright. Richard was missing the back-up from members of his fellowship back home. Perhaps he should not have undertaken this pilgrimage after all, as one member of his housegroup had advised him. His wife Linda had been generous to let him come on his own. She saw it as her contribution to his training as one of the worship leaders at his church. He realized he was missing Linda. Surely she would encourage him now to persevere and to trust in God speaking to him in some way. In fact, wasn't this what the beatitudes were all about: having faith and trust in the God Jesus revealed?

By the time Richard rejoined the group, they had moved on and were busy making up their own beatitudes: 'Blessed are you who read many books, for your mind shall be expanded' – that was Fiona's offering. Richard felt uncomfortable. This had nothing to do with Jesus' beatitudes!

Ian agreed and said that the provocative thing about the biblical beatitudes was that – unlike Fiona's effort – they were contrary to common experience. While Brenda loved this and saw it as a sign of hope, Fiona also remembered how difficult this could be: she told them how she had seen people in need being fobbed off with a reference to the beatitudes, as though their suffering there and then did not really matter.

Richard had had enough. 'Why do you always have to be so critical and negative? The Gospel encourages us to have faith in Jesus!'

'I agree,' said Laura, 'but surely the beatitudes show us how the message of Jesus is about the kingdom of God – the question is whether you think the kingdom of God is something to be entered after death or something to be built now.'

Julia smiled: 'And this is a huge question! I don't think it's an "either–or". Remember the scene in the synagogue from Luke's Gospel: Jesus reads from the scroll of Isaiah, and when all eyes are on him, he declares the prophetic words to be fulfilled.

The spirit of the Lord GOD is upon me,
because the LORD has anointed me;
he has sent me to bring good news to the oppressed,
to bind up the broken-hearted,
to proclaim liberty to the captives,
and release to the prisoners.
(Isaiah 61)

'So I think the beatitudes reflect the life Jesus led, urging us to create a community of the kingdom where such mercy is shown to those who are less fortunate, weak and poor. And there's quite a strong hint that this is what God's ultimate rule has in mind.'

Laura saw this as another way of describing what Latin American liberation theology called God's 'bias for the poor'. Richard found himself really appreciating what Julia had said because it firmly linked the words of the beatitudes with the person of Jesus. That way, it suddenly all made sense: Jesus had lived out the words of the beatitudes in his own life, and following him meant doing the same in order to change hearts and lives today.

As they were talking, they arrived at a little open air chapel near the church. Julia asked Richard to help with the preparation of the table for a communion service.

When it came to sharing the peace, Julia had a surprise in store for them. Rather than encouraging the group to shake hands, she offered them a small flask of oil and invited them to anoint each other with a sign of the cross on the forehead or on the palm of the hand. It was to be a sign of mutual blessing, a prayer for one another that could – literally – be felt.

Julia explained that the word 'Messiah' meant 'anointed one'; it was a title for Jesus who was blessed by God and thus prepared and called to live God's kingdom.

'As we are!' Richard added.

After they had anointed each other, it was very quiet. They passed the bread and wine around – 'in remembrance of him'. And they realized as never before that the beatitudes were about the community of Jesus to which they belonged, which nurtured and sustained them, and which called them to serve others.

As they were clearing up the table, it dawned on Ian that he hadn't been at all bothered any more about whether the beatitudes were all originally by Jesus. Somehow, that paled into insignificance beside the experience he had just had.

After the service, Laura found herself more encouraged than she had been for a long time in church. So often the Church presented itself either as quite detached from this world, even hostile to it, or as an uncritical provider of religious services of all kinds. The beatitudes offered a message which was both counter-cultural and affirming.

In her short address at the service, Julia had drawn attention to the radical nature of Jesus' ministry. He was radically inclusive of people, including those on the margins. Frequently, he accepted meal invitations and table fellowship with 'tax-collectors and sinners'. At the same time, he was radically demanding of everyone. Holding such inclusivity and demand in perfect balance was an art at which the Church often did not excel, Julia said. It came down either on the cruel judgemental side or on the vacuous soft side. Laura had never found the 'Jesus loves you – anything goes' attitude particularly inspiring. It might be comfortable and better at times than the preaching of hellfire and damnation, but it left the gospel rather toothless and pointless – and certainly not liberating. The kingdom was about Jesus loving, challenging and blessing people and about the grace and demand of the gospel realized in relationship to him. If only the Church took this on board, it could be so much more courageous and encouraging. She sighed.

Harold noted that it was nearly time for lunch. In the afternoon they would be recalling the miracle of the loaves and fishes at Tabgha. As he saw Julia leading the way to the refectory, he was pleased they would not have to be relying on miracles!

During lunch, Ian was busy reading up about Tabgha. 'Imagine,' he said, 'it was less than a century ago that they discovered the best preserved mosaic in Israel.'

'Oh yes, the one with the loaves and fishes, I've already seen lots of souvenirs with that motif!' said Brenda. 'And in fact,' Ian went on, 'the stone with the mosaic was originally the altar of an early Byzantine church.' As the bus drew up at Tabgha, Julia reminded them that they were visiting the site where the story of the Feeding of the Five Thousand was traditionally located.

Following other pilgrims, they entered the church which had been built in the 1930s over the site of two successive Byzantine churches. The pilgrims already in the church were gazing at a small piece of mosaic at the foot of a simple altar. When it was their turn to stand around the mosaic, Julia asked Bill to read Matthew's story of the Feeding (Matthew 14.13–21). He paused when he got to the verse: 'We have nothing here but five loaves and two fish.'

They looked intently at the two fish either side of a basket with pieces of bread which looked like communion wafers.

Harold mused how people could believe that this tiny amount of food could feed so many people – and with so much left over.

'And all ate and were filled; and they took up what was left over of the broken pieces, twelve baskets full.'

Outside again, they met up and Laura remembered the prayers of intercession they had had at the communion service earlier in the day. With the words of the beatitudes, they had prayed for the hungry to be filled. Would that this were as easy as in the Bible story, she thought. 'Well, it can be, if only we put our trust in Jesus. He worked miracles then and he still does now!' Richard responded.

'Oh, for goodness' sake, Richard,' Laura exclaimed. 'Are you saying that all those hungry people in the world could be fed if only Christians prayed harder?'

Julia intervened. 'Let's stop and think for a moment. The story of the Feeding of the Five Thousand is actually a really interesting example of a miracle story. And it is told in all four Gospels, even in different versions within the same Gospel. There, in addition, is the story of the Feeding of the Four Thousand, and many people argue that this is simply a different version of the five-thousand story. John's Gospel combines the feeding story with one of the "I am" sayings in which Jesus refers to himself as the bread. Anyway, what matters is the message of the story.'

'It's a great story for hungry people!' said Laura. Julia nodded and explained that this would certainly have made it a very attractive story for poor people. Richard pointed out the spiritual side of the message, seeing the story as a sign of what happens when people are with Jesus and trust in Jesus. When Bill said he thought of this during the communion service, Julia smiled to herself. The author of John's Gospel had also made that association. His story of the Feeding of the Five Thousand carries obvious sacramental overtones. And then there was the Old Testament connection with the manna from heaven, when the people received basketfuls.

Meanwhile, Harold was debating with himself whether to join the discussion. He wanted to know whether Julia thought this and other miracles really happened. Brenda always got a little nervous when he found it difficult to accept some of these Bible stories. But Brenda's reaction would be nothing compared to Richard's, whom Harold found rather intense. Eventually, Harold managed to speak to Julia on his own.

'You see,' said Harold, 'when I was a lad, I thought whatever was in the Bible was true, just as I believed in the tooth fairy. But as an adult, I've found it impossible to believe that all these stories just happened like that, with the miracles and so on. And quite honestly, I'm not sure that it matters, anyway.'

Julia felt that it did matter to Harold in some way, otherwise they wouldn't be having this conversation! But the importance and relevance of a story didn't depend only on whether 'it happened' or not. 'Of course, in a sense it doesn't matter at all to you or me what happened two thousand years ago. It wouldn't affect you and me now if those people had gone out to buy sandwiches rather than being fed by Jesus. But I don't think the Gospel stories simply want to tell us what happened at certain times and in certain places during Jesus' lifetime. They want to share the God they experience in Jesus Christ, they want to tell us true stories of Jesus.'

Fiona and Brenda joined them: 'So you do think the miracle stories are true stories?' Fiona asked Julia.

'Well, yes and no. I don't think a story is only true if what it describes happened in exactly that way. What makes the miracle stories true for me is that they want to tell us the truth about Jesus. For the Gospel writers that truth is not restricted to the Jesus who walked this earth but includes the risen Christ whose presence inspires them. So I suppose I have to say no, I don't think every miracle happened just as it's described in the Gospels. But every miracle story has a message. It describes something of God's being and will for the world and shows us Jesus acting as God's representative or agent.'

Brenda was curious: 'Don't the miracle stories prove that Jesus was God's Son? I know that doesn't work if you don't believe Jesus did miracles in the first place, but still.'

Fiona said she'd heard that for people at the time of Jesus, a miracle really wasn't such a big deal. 'They didn't have our idea of laws of nature that can't be broken,' she added. Harold was sceptical. Surely even people in Jesus' time didn't think it was normal for food to multiply!

'You're certainly right there, Harold,' Julia responded. 'It wasn't normal – but it wasn't unique, either. There were other people around at the time of Jesus who were said to perform miracles. There was a certain expectation that people in touch with the divine, certain holy people, would be able to do that. Think of Old Testament stories, too: Elijah, for instance, provides a poor widow with an endless bottle of oil and raises her son from the dead. The whole concept of laws of nature wasn't born until much, much later.'

'But what about miracles today, then? Some Christians are pretty keen on that,' Harold persisted.

'You'll have to make up your own minds about that.' Julia was reluctant to be drawn. 'But let me say this. I was thinking while we were in the chapel at Tabgha how everyone crowded round the famous mosaic of the loaves and fishes. But actually, there was a much more beautiful mosaic of wildlife of the region on other parts of the floor. No-one took much notice of it. And I think it's the same for miracle stories in our lives. People concentrate on the ins and outs of the so-called "miracle" and disregard the rich story around it. As though God were only to be found in miraculous acts, not in the day-to-day things: for example, when someone shows forgiveness after an act of violence, when dogged research leads to the development of an effective drug, or when a carer's discipline and faithfulness enables a sick person to be looked after at home, and so on.'

Brenda was taken aback at this unmiraculous interpretation. And yet she was also moved when she applied this understanding of God's working to the lives of various people she knew.

'And now it's going to be a miracle if we get home in time for dinner,' Harold exclaimed, looking at his watch. The other part of the group had wandered over to the Church of the Primacy nearby. It was the place where Jesus was said to have appeared to his disciples after Easter, prepared breakfast for them and told Peter to tend the flock. It was certainly another real miracle, Julia thought, that weak Peter, who had denied Jesus, became such a formidable leader in the early Church.

* * *

In the meeting room that night, Julia introduced a hand-out on miracles to provide a brief overview.

1. Different kinds of miracle stories told about Jesus
   - *gift miracles* – the feeding miracle is one of them, as is the story of changing the water into wine at Cana (John 2)
   - *deliverance miracles* – for instance the stilling of the storm
   - *epiphanies* – the transfiguration
   - and the healing miracles are strictly speaking of two different kinds:
     - *therapies*
     - *exorcisms*

59

2. The source of the miracle – the source of the stories
   The miracle stories are told of Jesus – God hardly ever appears directly active in them. A typical trait in Jesus' ministry is the role he often ascribes to the faith of the person who is helped by the miracle. Where there is faith, Jesus says, 'Your faith has healed you'; when the disciples do not show enough faith (stilling of the storm, for instance) they are reprimanded for that.

   Miracle stories were and are good stories to tell. Many scholars see the miracles as a product both of the memory of Jesus' charismatic ministry and of the retelling and reinterpretation of his life in the light of his resurrection.

3. The interpretation of the miracle stories
   The interpretation of miracles is most clearly worked out in John's Gospel. John speaks of 'signs', so for him the miracle stories become transparent for an underlying spiritual truth.

   In stories from the synoptic Gospels – for instance, gift stories or healings – the miracle stories can be seen to express God's compassion and protest against suffering.

Julia looked around. Laura saw the political relevance of the last point and got a lot out of it. It appealed to her to be able to hold on to the miracle stories without having to subscribe to a mythical view of the world.

Richard, by contrast, was really struggling. He found it hard to live with these interpretations. The idea that some miracle stories were actually a reflection of the risen Christ and not about Jesus in his lifetime caused him particular trouble. In fact, he couldn't accept it at all, but he felt too tired to say anything. He always felt like the odd one out, and it was not a comfortable position to be in.

Julia realized it was time to call it a day. So they prayed.

Lord Jesus Christ,
you have called blessed those who are seeking and longing.
Fill our hearts and lives with your vision and compassion,

so that we may join in your labours for this world.
For your love's sake.
Amen.

Questions for discussion

1. Which beatitudes have you encountered in your life?

2. What is your reaction to the scene of the members of the group anointing each other? Can you think of occasions or situations where Christians should be encouraged to bless each other?

3. When Harold asked, 'What about miracles today?' Julia replied, 'You'll have to make up your own minds.' What do you think?

8

A Journey to Banyas

Early next morning a rather bleary-eyed group got on the bus. They
had stayed up on the previous night discussing Jesus' miracles.
And it was all Fiona's fault. She had asked what 'faith' meant when
Jesus said in the healing stories, 'Your faith has made you well.'
Richard had been quite certain that 'faith' meant faith in Jesus, but
Fiona thought that it should be understood in a much wider sense as
referring to a person's confidence.

Fiona's view prompted the group to wonder whether Jesus' healing miracles were the result of a psychosomatic effect he had on
people. Julia pointed out, however, that that was definitely not how
the Gospel writers saw the situation. She reminded them how often
Jesus addressed sick people directly in order to get them to say
what they wanted. The whole point was not that the healing was an
objective miracle or the result of someone subjectively feeling
good about themselves. Rather, people found a voice, were raised
up and set free from their affliction because they were with Jesus,
because Jesus related to them and because they sought his
company.

Richard protested that people would only have gone to Jesus
because of who they thought he was – the Messiah, the Son of God.
The women in the group, however, thought that the miracles had
less to do with doctrine and more with people putting their trust in
Jesus. Julia backed this up by translating the Greek word for *faith*
as *trust* rather than *belief.* The group acknowledged that amazing
and unpredictable things seemed to happen when people met Jesus
– or was it when Jesus met people? With these thoughts they had
finally called it a day.

The bus was now taking them north towards the snow-capped
Mount Hermon in Lebanon. They were on their way to Banyas, the
site of Caesarea Philippi where Jesus asked his disciples what other
people and they themselves thought of him. On the journey, Julia
wanted to talk with them about Jesus' parables. She had asked each

of them to choose a favourite parable, and the choices proved astonishing. For each had chosen a parable which expressed something of what they saw as the quintessential message of Jesus.

The Good Samaritan[1] and the Prodigal Son[2] were Harold's and Brenda's favourites respectively. Since, for Harold, the Christian faith was about offering unqualified help to others, the Good Samaritan was an obvious choice for him. Brenda loved the parable of the Prodigal Son because it spoke so vividly of God's generous love.

It was this love which Laura also found in the parable of the Labourers in the Vineyard.[3] Brenda and Harold thought this was a rather prickly parable, since everyone would naturally sympathize with those who worked all day rather than with those who got the same wage for only an hour's work. But Laura loved this parable ever since she heard it interpreted as a story of God's justice. It meant that God gave to everyone a day's wage, which is what they needed to live, rather than giving them what they appeared to deserve. 'And that', she affirmed, 'is the standard for God's kingdom!' In short, she had enthusiasm for the kingdom values discussed at a recent 'peace and justice' conference written all over her. The others had to smile.

'All right,' Fiona said, 'you can smile at my choice, too. I picked the Judgement of the Nations.[4] I have to admit, of course, that with my inter-faith leanings, the idea that Christ is in everyone appeals to me. And I believe strongly that, in the end, it's not belief but actions that separate the sheep from the goats.'

Julia pointed out that the parables mentioned so far were all unique to either Luke or Matthew. 'Don't worry,' said Richard, 'I can widen the field. My parable – about the sower whose seeds fall on different types of ground[5] – is in the first three Gospels. And it's so wonderfully clear and really expresses what happens when the word is preached.' He smiled shyly. 'It explains why it isn't necessarily my fault when I share the gospel with someone to no effect!'

'Mm,' said Fiona, 'I can see why you like it, Richard. It really is straightforward. But somehow, because Jesus himself explains its precise meaning, it's a bit too neat for me. You see, what I love about many of the parables is their unexpected twists: the way they draw you into a story, turn something on its head and catch you out.'

Brenda supposed that in a sense Jesus was like a storyteller. The others laughed – Jesus, they insisted, *was* a storyteller! After Julia had explained that telling parables was one of the mainstays of his teaching, Bill volunteered his parable, which, he said, contained the essential gospel message. It was the violent parable of the Wicked Tenants,[6] in which the tenants in the vineyard kill the owner's son. And its appeal for Bill was that it illuminated both Jesus' fate and purpose, and the realities of the world. 'There are so many people represented in this parable,' he said. 'Prophets of the Old Testament, those of us who reject Jesus, and even Jesus himself.'

'I see what you mean,' said Fiona, 'but we must be careful with this parable. It can appear to justify anti-Semitism by laying the blame for Jesus' death firmly at the door of the Jews.' Bill was horrified by this suggestion. The point he had wanted to make had nothing to do with it.

Julia intervened. 'I know what you mean, Fiona, but don't confuse anti-Semitism with anti-Judaism. Anti-Semitism is racism against Jews per se while anti-Judaism is a theological position opposed to Jewish faith and thought. And yes, that can feed into anti-Semitism. We'll talk about who might have been responsible for what in the crucifixion story when we're in Jerusalem.'

Bill looked confused. 'Of course the Jews rejected Jesus but that doesn't mean I'm in favour of persecuting Jews!' he replied. 'I think they stand for each one of us when we reject Jesus.' Fiona mumbled that that wasn't good enough, using Jews to represent Christian sinfulness when Jesus himself was a Jew, but the conversation moved on as everyone turned to Ian expectantly.

Ian laughed nervously and said he had chosen a no-frills parable, the one about the kingdom of heaven being like a mustard seed.[7]

Several of the group admitted to not quite knowing the story. 'There isn't much of a story in this one,' said Ian, 'just a reminder that the tiny mustard seed turns into a huge tree in which many birds build their nests. I can imagine Jesus making such pithy statements about God's kingdom.'

Julia pointed out that they had lumped together different types of stories, comparisons, aphorisms, example stories, etc. and called them all *parables*. 'How can we know what they all mean?' asked Brenda. Richard's parable was easy enough, since it came with Jesus' explanation, but the other parables didn't.

Ian said that a lot of the parables were about the kingdom of God and they were introduced as such: 'the kingdom of God is like . . .'. But that didn't help Brenda understand all the details of the parables.

Julia came to her aid. 'Analysing every detail is not the point, Brenda. Some of the parables are structured a bit like a joke. The main part simply sets the scene to draw you in before the punchline is delivered. That's all there is to it. Other parables clearly are allegories, like Richard's parable of the sower. Here, every element in the story contributes to the meaning of the whole.'

When Ian, forever interested in authenticity, wondered whether Jesus himself had used allegories, Julia acknowledged that some of the stories might be attempts by the Church to spell out secret messages which they believed Jesus was communicating to his disciples through his parables. 'But that only goes to underline what is virtually undisputed, namely that Jesus did use parables widely in his teaching.'

Ian then wondered why Jesus veiled his message with stories rather than expressing what he wanted to say more directly. At this, Fiona shook her head, and Julia encouraged her to respond. Fiona was the only person in the group with a strong literary vein. She spoke movingly of Jesus as the poet who was so very important to her and whose words created a God-reality by drawing the hearer into a story, invariably about the everyday world, and often ending with a twist.

65

Harold broke the silence which followed: 'Julia, which is *your* favourite parable?' Julia offered a parable from John's Gospel, the one of the vine and the branches.[8] Suddenly she laughed and said, 'I'd better admit that I only chose this one because we haven't had anything so far from John's Gospel, and it shows how Jesus uses Old Testament imagery. Just think of Isaiah's Vineyard song.'[9]

Then Laura had an idea. 'What about the "I am" sayings in John's Gospel – you know "I am the shepherd", or "I am the bread of life"? Are they a kind of parable as well?'

At this point the bus swung into a car park. They had arrived at Banyas and Julia smiled. 'Excellent timing, Laura,' she said. 'The "I am" sayings are metaphors which John uses to say something about what matters most to him – not the kingdom as in the first three Gospels, but who Jesus is. And that question has a lot to do with this place.'

Banyas was a place of pools and rocks, the source of the River Jordan. Tourists and sightseers had been there long before the rise of the Roman empire. Other gods, Syrian and Greek, had been worshipped there. And under Roman rule, in the territory of one of Herod's sons, it was a very worldly centre, Caesarea Philippi, considered to be the birthplace of the god Pan. At that time, the top of the hill glistened with the white marble of a temple built to Caesar, a sign of the power and divinity of Rome. Against this backdrop of many religions, Jesus put the question to his disciples, 'Who do you say I am?'

Bill read a few verses of the story from Matthew's Gospel, Matthew 16.13–20, where Peter called Jesus the Messiah, meaning God's Anointed, and Son of God.

Julia invited them to reflect on the answer they would have given. Richard was deeply moved. He still remembered how he came to faith as a young adult and made that decisive step to believe in Jesus as the Son of God. And here he was, at the very place where Peter had confessed that same faith. For him, Jesus was Lord, the Son of God.

Meanwhile, Brenda was holding Harold's hand. She did not

want him to feel out of it. But Harold was quite happy. It was a serene place and he felt Jesus was a good friend to him. Brenda's mind was racing. What did she think of Jesus? Of course, he was divine, but she also loved the human side of him. He was the Son of God, but also a real human being with joys and tears.

Doubts and slight annoyance filled Fiona's mind. She could not think of Jesus in those categories of Son of God or Messiah. Rabbi, perhaps, was a better one, relating to his teaching ministry.

As they wandered around the rocks, they wondered what people today would or in fact did say about Jesus.

Julia picked up a small stone and threw it into one of the still pools. The stone vanished from sight immediately but the waves and ripples worked their way through the pool. 'This', said Julia, 'is how I'd like you to think about all those titles we give to Jesus. Jesus whom we don't see any more, made waves, and we put names to those waves.'

'Titles like Rabbi or Master make a lot of sense,' said Fiona, 'but when it comes to Son of God . . .'

'Are you saying Jesus wasn't the Son of God?' Richard enquired. 'Are you saying Jesus didn't *think* he was the Son of God?'

Fiona gave his question a very blunt answer: 'Surely he would have been a mental case if he had *thought* that he was the Son of God!'

Julia responded quickly that she thought Jesus' Jewish faith would not have allowed him to perceive himself in that way – didn't he once rebuke someone who called him good by saying that only God was good?! 'He seems to have called himself "Son of Man" but we're not sure whether Jesus had a particular meaning in mind,' she continued. The striking thing was how, following Peter's confession, Mark and Matthew immediately launched into thoughts of the passion.

Julia invited them to join in an Affirmation of Faith taken from Philippians 2.

'Let us affirm our faith in Jesus Christ the Son of God.'

Though he was divine,
he did not cling to equality with God,
but emptied himself.
Taking the form of a slave,
he was born in human likeness.
He humbled himself
and was obedient to death,
even the death of the cross.
Therefore God has raised him on high,
and given him the name above every name:
that at the name of Jesus
every knee should bow,
and every voice proclaim that Jesus Christ is Lord,
to the glory of God the Father.
Amen.

* * *

It was time for one last evening session in Galilee before returning to Jerusalem the next day.

Julia was keen to summarize two issues, the parables and the titles of Jesus. It was Ian who had asked about the parables, in particular whether they were unique to Jesus, and Julia was pleased to answer him.

'You can find parables in the broadest sense in the Old Testament – from proverbs and riddles to story parables. The parables are so embedded in the Jesus tradition that there is little doubt that Jesus used them in his teaching. In this Jesus was not unique. Rabbis commonly used parables.

'Some of the parables we find in the Gospels may not originate with Jesus. For instance, the parable of the rich man and Lazarus is basically a widespread Egyptian story.[10] We don't know for certain whether Jesus used this story or whether it was a parable inserted later into the Jesus tradition.

'One thing is obvious, there is a Galilean flavour to Jesus' parables. The scenes Jesus describes reveal people trying to make a living, hoping to better themselves financially, living the faith with more or less integrity and dedication and facing all the tensions, contrasts and prejudices of the society he observed and knew so well. Above all, Jesus aims in his parables to invite people to take a fresh look at life and God's kingdom. If, therefore, some of the behaviour described is unexpected or exaggerated, it only serves to highlight something important on the canvas of daily life.

'But what is a parable? When I spoke of parables in the broadest sense I meant that the "parable" can take a host of different literary forms.

'There are *similitude stories* which liken one thing to another. For instance, Ian's parable about the mustard seed which begins "the kingdom of God is like . . .".

'There are *example stories* which provoke people to act in a particular way – for instance, Harold's parable of the Good Samaritan which answers the question "Who is my neighbour?"

'There are *extended metaphors* like the parable of the Prodigal Son where Jesus makes use of the father-metaphor for God – which is why the parable should really be called the parable of the Merciful Father!

'And there are *allegories*, like Richard's Sower or the Wicked Tenants.

'Is this sort of classification really useful? Well, it is, because the thing we're most likely to do when we put our Bible study hats on is to overinterpret the parables! And one of the most common ways of doing this is interpreting all the parables as allegories and giving special meaning to each detail of the story. In fact, by doing this, we're likely to miss the main point altogether. On the other hand, it would be quite wrong and certainly unhelpful to say there was only one correct way of interpreting parables. There is no single correct interpretation and one of the marvels of the parables is that they do speak to us directly and set us free to reflect for ourselves on our life and faith.

69

'Now then, let's talk about the special titles for Jesus.'

'One of them is *prophet*. A lot of his contemporaries seem to have regarded Jesus as a prophet. That's not surprising, for several reasons. There were a good number of prophets at the time of Jesus, not least those plotting rebellion against Rome. This is what might have led Jesus into trouble when the Jewish authorities saw him as a false prophet – a prophet nonetheless. The things Jesus did, his healings, his entry into Jerusalem, give him the appearance of a prophet. And when he associates himself with prophetic figures such as Elijah or John the Baptist, that suggests that he did indeed see himself as a prophet.'

'Then we also find Jesus addressed as *Rabbi*, or *Master* or *Teacher*. This is a deferential way of addressing someone and refers to his authoritative teaching. There are many stories of Jesus teaching in the synagogue. The title "rabbi" doesn't mean that he was formally a rabbi. The title was used quite loosely at the time of Jesus for someone who was a recognized teacher.'

'Jesus, the *Lord*. From a confessional point of view, this is the first really interesting title for us Christians. When we say "Jesus is Lord", we are making a credal statement. However, this is not necessarily the case when the title is used in the New Testament. You see, there are two angles to this. On the one hand, especially in Paul's letters, "Lord" clearly implies Jesus' divinity and refers to the living risen Jesus. But the Greek word for "Lord", *Kyrios*, can be used both for God and for a male human authority figure. Therefore, some translations of the New Testament simply use the word "sir" for instances where Jesus is addressed as *kyrie*. By contrast, when we say or sing "Kyrie eleison", "Lord, have mercy", in worship, we appeal to the risen living Christ.'

'Jesus is *Son of God*. This is a clear statement of faith and of key importance for Christians. The two main sources for this are the baptism stories and the way John's Gospel speaks of Jesus.

'In the baptism stories the voice of God calls Jesus a "son" in a much more specific sense than being one of God's children. Luke's Gospel in particular has given rise to the interpretation that the point of baptism is God's adoption of Jesus. Sonship then is the prime definition of Jesus' relationship to God.

'In John's Gospel Jesus persistently refers to God as the Father with whom he is one. The first chapter of John's Gospel underpins this with a highly developed theology of Jesus' divinity. The idea of Jesus' sonship thus describes an essential part of Jesus' being, whereas in the synoptic Gospels the idea of sonship is much more related to Jesus' mission.

'There are other examples in the first three Gospels where understanding Jesus as the Son of God plays a definitive role. For instance, the allegory of the Wicked Tenants implies that Jesus is the Son of God.

'In the trial scenes, the Son of God title features in the blasphemy charges against Jesus. It is uncertain whether this is a later Christian interpretation or whether Jesus' exorcisms led to the accusation that he called himself the Son of God.

'It is difficult if not impossible to say what Jesus thought of himself. But the Gospels do give us the impression that he had a special sense of closeness to God. Who can tell to what extent, in Jesus' experience, this went beyond a human mystical relationship with God?'

'Jesus and the *Son of Man*. This is one of the most discussed titles for Jesus – yet it is the one that Jesus most certainly used to refer to himself! What does it mean? You can take your pick. Some scholars think it is little more than a modest way of saying "I", while others see it as a reference to the "Son of Man" of apocalyptic times,[11] and others again that Jesus chose the title "Son of Man" for himself so that he could fill an undetermined title with new meaning. It's interesting that the early Church did not continue using this title. To my mind, this suggests it was not something introduced by the first Christians but a title Jesus actually used for himself – though we may never know with certainty what he meant by it.'

'It is worth mentioning that Jesus is referred to on several occasions as *Son of David*. Although Jesus appears to have rejected the title (Mark 12.35–7), it seems to be firmly anchored in the Jesus tradition and is connected to the idea that he was the Messiah, who was expected to be a descendant of David.'

'So, Jesus as the *Messiah*. "Christ" is the Greek translation for this Hebrew title. Literally, it means "the anointed". In my favourite passage from Luke's Gospel, Luke 4.16–21, Jesus refers to himself with messianic words drawn from Isaiah 61.

'I used to think that one of the decisive questions about Jesus was whether he was *the* Messiah. But at the time of Jesus, there were lots of different expectations of what this Messiah might be like, including politically and militarily highly charged ones. Jesus certainly seems to have shied away from those associations. Think of the Banyas scene in which he rebukes Peter for not understanding that the path of suffering was integral to his particular "messianic" vocation.

'Jesus generally appears to avoid the title "Messiah", not only, perhaps, because of the associations he does not share but also because of the related dangers which ultimately led to the cross in Jerusalem.

'And it is Jerusalem to which *we* are heading tomorrow, too!

'Let us pray.'

Lord Jesus Christ,
storytelling Son of God
gracious Friend,
help us to listen to your story and to the stories you told,
hold us that we may look to you and understand you more deeply,
lead us into the mystery of your kingdom among us,
for your love's sake.
Amen.

Questions for discussion

1. What is your favourite parable? Why? What does it mean for you?

2. Who do people today say Jesus is? Who do you say he is? Is there a new title for Jesus which you might find helpful?

3. Take each of the titles of Jesus in this chapter and discuss what they mean to you in the context of life and worship.

9

The Journey to Jerusalem

'Are you sure we've got everything?' Brenda enquired anxiously of Harold as the luggage was heaved onto the bus. Fiona quipped: 'Doesn't it say somewhere that you should take no bag for your journey and that one tunic is enough?'

'Well, I'm not Jesus and when I think of where his journey ended, I can't say I'm sorry!' This was Laura. They were on their way from Tiberias to Jerusalem. Or, as Julia explained, they were continuing their journey from Banyas, alias Caesarea Philippi, through Galilee and via Jericho to Jerusalem.

Ian wondered why Jericho. Was it an important staging-post for pilgrims on their way to Jerusalem?

'Not as such,' Bill replied unexpectedly. 'You remember we talked about this on our way north. It's just that, because Galilean pilgrims would have wanted to avoid Samaria, they would have stuck to the Jordan Valley and passed through Jericho on their way.' The others looked impressed!

For Bill, this was an important journey. At Caesarea Philippi, they had recalled Peter's confession and his rebuke by Jesus. Now he felt how the cross was casting its shadow more and more on Jesus' life. Increasingly, the Gospels were mentioning Jesus' impending suffering. Jerusalem was like a magnet, drawing Jesus to itself.

A few hours later, the bus dropped them off at Bethany, just outside Jerusalem. Julia asked them each to think of people who were walking a difficult but inevitable or necessary path in their lives. So they walked in silence for part of the two miles towards Jerusalem.

Laura and Ian thought of the prisoners of conscience they supported through Amnesty International – people who spoke out for the truth although they knew it would get them into trouble. Fiona remembered her friend Marion who was going through a separation that she did not wish for. Marion was terrified of living on her

74

own and bringing up the children alone but she knew there was no alternative for her. Richard thought admiringly of Ben, one of the lay church leaders who felt called to full-time ministry overseas but was anxious about giving up a good job and a high standard of living. Thinking of them praying together about it, Richard saw parallels to the Gethsemane experience – though at least he, Richard, had not fallen asleep as they had prayed!

Brenda and Harold both thought of Harold's friend Henry, who was to undergo painful cancer treatment although he felt all right at the moment.

It was a thoughtful group drawing closer to Jerusalem who went halfway down the Mount of Olives to the Dominus Flevit Church. Through the glass window above the altar they enjoyed a panoramic view of the Old City. Julia asked Bill to read the Palm Sunday story of Jesus' entry into Jerusalem from the version in Luke's Gospel, 19.29–40 – although it's the one Gospel which makes no reference to palms.

Laura was very struck by the passage about Jesus weeping over the city. 'It's lovely to hear of Jesus weeping over the city but the passage is also dark with those violent prophecies of Jerusalem's destruction. And I had never associated this passage with the Palm Sunday story.'

'I know what you mean,' said Julia. 'It goes to show that we often read our Bible in a piecemeal fashion. But once you've been here you don't forget. This church is, I think, one of the most memorable in Jerusalem, and as its name indicates, it commemorates the place where Jesus wept over the city. That's why it's tear-shaped!'

Ian, as usual, was the most rational about it all. He was mainly interested in whether Jesus' Palm Sunday entry to Jerusalem was really his *first* visit to Jerusalem during his public ministry.

Julia told him that he had John's Gospel on his side. 'John presents Jesus cleansing the Temple in Jerusalem right at the beginning of his ministry, but there were probably theological reasons for that. John wanted to put down a marker from the start against the practice of Judaism. If Jesus did pay several visits to Jerusalem before "Palm Sunday", we don't know anything about them.'

Richard was left to his own thoughts again. He hated the uncertainties about the Bible stories which Julia seemed to keep highlighting. He had come on the pilgrimage to see with his own eyes, to be reassured. And yes, there was something amazing about being here. But he felt that rather than his grasp of the faith being tightened, it was in fact slipping. He would never be able to admit that – great budding worship leader that he was! – to his house-group, and perhaps not even to Linda. He wished that his sarcasm could make him snap out of this dark mood.

Close to the city walls, Julia read some verses from Psalm 122:

I was glad when they said to me, 'Let us go to the house of the Lord!' Our feet are standing within your gates, O Jerusalem.
O pray for the peace of Jerusalem: 'May they prosper who love you. Peace be within your walls and security within your towers.'

'I want these verses to be with us as we explore Jesus' story in Jerusalem,' said Julia. 'We must not forget that this is a special and holy city for Christians, Jews and Muslims. It tells us much about the past but it is also a vibrant city where people live and work. So when we think of Jesus' entering the city on Palm Sunday, it is worth remembering that today many people who live outside Jerusalem cannot freely enter because of the political and military restrictions. And I don't need to remind you of the bloodshed and violence, the conflicts and the failed peace plans.

'With all the security guards around, you'll be very much aware of this as we go to the Western Wall of the Temple.'

When they arrived in the Western Wall area, they found not only other pilgrims and tourists but also many Jewish people praying. Fiona was fascinated by the juxtaposition of the holy sites, for high above the Western Wall was the imposing Dome of the Rock, venerated by Muslims as the place where Abraham prepared to sacrifice Isaac. The Western Wall, in turn, was revered by Jews as the only remaining wall of the last Temple. The vast space in front of it accommodated many worshippers. During his time in Jerusalem, Jesus taught in the Temple. It was hard to imagine that great building, from the one wall left standing.

Brenda was trying to take it all in when she heard Ian ask about Temple stories in the Gospels. 'The Presentation of Christ in the Temple', she called out. She loved the story of old Simeon and Anna greeting little Jesus. And Richard added the account of the 12-year-old Jesus in the Temple. Julia nodded. 'Yes, and interestingly both passages are only found in Luke's Gospel.[1] But there is also the story we have already mentioned, the cleansing of the Temple. You'll find that in all four Gospels, although John located it at the beginning of Jesus' ministry rather than at the end.'

Now that was a story Brenda was unhappy about. Of course she understood Jesus being angry about the irreverent trading going on, but the idea of Jesus whipping people out of the Temple made her uncomfortable. When she said as much to Fiona and Laura, Fiona understood how she felt but Laura was glad that Jesus wasn't as wimpish as the Church when it came to things he felt strongly about.

Julia meanwhile had asked Richard to read the story of the cleansing of the Temple from Matthew's Gospel.[2] Brenda was confused. There was no mention of a whip of cords! Then Julia suggested having a look at the version from John's Gospel.[3] 'John's story is more detailed than Matthew, Mark and Luke. He even describes the sort of animals that were on offer in the Temple grounds for sacrifice. John is the only one who indicates that Jesus made a whip of cords, and because in our minds we muddle up John's story with the versions in the other Gospels, we think that they all say that Jesus was whipping the people out of the Temple. In fact, he uses a whip in John's Gospel, and there he is not whipping people, but driving out the cattle with the whip of cords.'

'That's really helpful, Julia,' said Brenda, 'and it still shows that Jesus was pretty determined – but without hitting people!'

'But what was he so determined about?' queried Ian. 'Was it a political claim, an ill-fated attempt at revolution, or some sort of concern for religious purity?'

'There is a word of Scripture from the prophets against trading in the Temple,' said Richard, 'So Jesus was simply being faithful to God's Word!'

'I've heard that Jesus was outraged because poor people were being ripped off by the traders!' said Laura.

They all turned expectantly to Julia, as though she were the referee between these divergent interpretations. 'What can I say? It's a difficult one and I think there is something in what each of you has said. If you start with Jesus' entry into Jerusalem, there is the possibility of at least some political implication. He has the authority to commandeer the donkey but he presents himself as humble. Richard mentioned the prophets, and it's Zechariah who speaks of the coming one riding on a donkey.[4] Some will want to argue that this word of Scripture has itself shaped the story. There is very little indication that the entry into Jerusalem and the cleansing of the Temple were major events in the life of the city. There would have been thousands of pilgrims, including lots of country folk, filling the streets in preparation for the Passover, so don't imagine a quiet city dominated by the presence of Jesus. It's worth noting that it is actually Jesus' fellow pilgrims who are hailing him, not the city people. During the festival that urban–rural divide could lead to tensions – that's why the Roman prefect was there. There's a sense in which Jesus becomes the victim of some of these structural conflicts between Jews and Romans, between city dwellers and country folk, and between the common people and the Jewish aristocracy.

'As for the claim that Jesus was a revolutionary – I think that's no more than a romantic idea. Even if you assume that the Gospel writers would have toned down any overt political aggression, there is very little to support such a notion. If anything, Jesus always seems to emphasize that it's God who will make the kingdom come, not us.

'The Book of Zechariah closes with a description of how trading in the house of the Lord comes to an end when the new age dawns. Jesus may well have been motivated by that conviction, and also – as Laura suggested – by his dismay that poor people were being exploited when they bought their animals from the traders at the Temple.'

As Ian was standing in front of the ancient historic wall, he was struck by the layers of meaning and significance surrounding him: there was history and politics, there was biblical tradition, there was worship. Ian was not given to religious sentiment but there was something stirring in him that surprised him.

Suddenly it was time to go.

'We're going to leave the Western Wall and the Old City,' said Julia. 'The bus will pick us up outside the Dung Gate and take us to where we have a panoramic view of the city. There's more to think about before we go to the hostel.'

Later, as they took in the view, Julia read them Jesus' lament over Jerusalem. '"Jerusalem, Jerusalem, the city that kills the prophets and stones those who are sent to it! . . . See, your house is left to you, desolate."[5] And then,' she added, 'Jesus foretells the destruction of the Temple. The passage reveals great love for Jerusalem and for the Temple, too, but also a deep sense of the painful emergence of a new age.'

'Oh, it's these apocalyptic texts! Is there really any substance to them?' This was sceptical Ian. Richard replied hotly, 'I'm sure they're not just there to make up the pages!'

'Calm down, you two,' said Julia. 'These passages which we find in the first three Gospels[6] are actually really difficult to interpret, and Christian sects through the ages have read into them what they liked. You can read them to understand better the aspects of Jesus which we don't like to think about so much, and you can also read them as a reflection of the traumas which befell the early Christian communities. The descriptions of betrayal and having to stand trial speak vividly of that.

'But let me just come back to the Temple. One thing is

fundamental for Jesus' apocalypse, and that is the destruction of the Temple. Jesus' criticism of the Temple almost certainly played an important part in the passion story.'

While Ian was fascinated by all this, Brenda was struggling to work out what the apocalypse had to do with her attempts to be a Christian in Farnley. 'Can you help us with that, Julia?' she asked.

'Yes, of course,' Julia replied. 'You know Jesus had a base with his friends Mary, Martha and Lazarus in Bethany. Well, in the same way we're going back to our accommodation now so that we can talk about everything.' 'How can that have been Jesus' base if, as you claim, John's Gospel invented that he was in Jerusalem more than once?' Richard asked sharply. The others looked uncomfortable at the tone of his question. 'You're quite right,' Julia replied calmly. 'That particular tradition is from John's Gospel, though Mark also mentions that Jesus went out to Bethany after the cleansing of the Temple.[7] Luke's Gospel, by contrast, says that Jesus spent the night on the Mount of Olives.[8] But we're now going to the pilgrims' hostel for the night. I think that we all need the rest.'

Richard blushed and apologized. Oh dear, he hadn't meant to be like that. Things had just got on top of him.

* * *

'Let me talk to you about Apocalypse Now,' Julia introduced the evening session to everyone's amusement.

'I used the term today for passages in the first three Gospels where Jesus speaks of a time to come. The word "apocalypse" comes from a Greek word meaning "reveal".

'After the cleansing of the Temple, Jesus told his disciples that the Temple was going to be destroyed. They wanted to know more about this and it's interesting to note that the Mount of Olives is the place where Jesus speaks to them about the last things. Again, in Zechariah, the Mount of Olives plays a prominent part in the events of the last days.[9]

'We can't go into all the details of the rich imagery that Jesus uses, but it is important to be aware that the so-called "synoptic apocalypse"[10] is firmly rooted in the genre of apocalyptic literature and in the apocalyptic passages of the Old Testament and later intertestamental writings. I think what is projected into the future reflects these Jewish writings and historic events of the past as well as experiences of the first Christians between Jesus' lifetime and the finalizing of the Gospels. So the coming trials and tribulations that Jesus describes include scenes of persecution and appearances of false Messiahs. All these reflect the situation of the early Christian community. The desolating sacrilege in the Temple recalls a second-century BCE event in which the Temple was desecrated. The cosmic signs are typical symbolism for an apocalypse, and the coming of the Son of Man is a theme from the Book of Daniel and other writings.

'Sayings influenced by apocalyptic thought are found throughout Jesus' teaching, and I firmly believe this is a side of Jesus which we often don't take seriously enough. The expectation of the imminent coming of God's kingdom would have shaped Jesus' thinking. All the exhortations to watchfulness should be seen in that light.

'And this is where apocalyptic thought becomes relevant to us.

'One of the very clear characteristics of Jesus' apocalyptic tradition is the emphasis on the impossibility of knowing when these things are going to happen. The disciples' question about this remains deliberately unanswered. In the little parable, the doorkeeper doesn't know when the master of the house will come. Similarly, Jesus' followers can only be watchful and prepared.

'There is therefore a spiritual and an ethical implication in Jesus' apocalyptic teaching. God cannot be predicted, calculated or fenced in. Both God's salvation and God's judgement will include unexpected people. There is no substitute for faithful watchfulness which puts the kingdom values first. Matthew's parable of the Judgement of the Nations is probably the best illustration of this. It affirms that Jesus had been present where no-one had expected him, in the least of his brothers and sisters.

81

'There is a keen sense of urgency in Jesus' ministry, teaching and preaching. It isn't hectic but it has no time for superficial nonsense, either. Instead, it invariably goes to the heart of the matter. As a man of his time, I think Jesus did have apocalyptic expectations of the end of the world, and this would have shaped his thinking. Hence his emphatic teaching on the day of judgement, in line with the prophets and John the Baptist, with its powerful impact on his hearers' minds.

'Do we in the twenty-first century have to share those expectations about the dawning of God's kingdom in time and space?

'Some, who like the first Christians were disappointed that Jesus did not return straight away, think that the kingdom is simply delayed in time. Others hold that the kingdom of God is not about space and time in the first place but about God's rule and the life it both offers and demands. Certainly there are sayings of Jesus indicating both a present and future expectation of God's kingdom.

'What seems to me to matter most is the inescapable urgency about the kingdom of God. It can't wait, nothing is more important.

'Well, I hope that was helpful, although it may raise many more questions. I think there is something about these apocalyptic passages which sounds quite unreal. But the more I think about them, the more relevant and real they seem. They speak vividly of the unexpectedness of God, and their emphasis on the times of trial is a sad reflection on the way we run this world.

'So, on this first night back in Jerusalem, I would like to offer a prayer for peace by the Anglican Bishop in Jerusalem, Riah Abu Al-Assal':[11]

Almighty and most merciful Father, lover of justice and of peace; direct the minds and wills of those who are called to govern the peoples of Israel and Palestine, where your Son our Lord Jesus Christ walked, preached and went on healing the wounds of those around him.
May they become instruments of your peace.

*May they have regard to your laws and all that would protect
your beautiful image in your creatures.
Enable them to work for peace, founded on truth, justice and
righteousness.
We ask this through him who was lifted up in Jerusalem on the
wood of the cross,
that he may draw all people to himself, the same Jesus Christ
our Lord. Amen.*

Questions for discussion

1. Richard hated the uncertainties about the Bible story. How do
   you react to Julia's approach to the Gospel narratives?

2. Jesus drove the traders out of the Temple. What things in
   today's Church would he drive out?

3. Read Mark 13. Why do you think it was important to the first
   readers of the Gospel and what sense can you make of it for
   Christian faith today?

10

The Passion

Since being back in Jerusalem, Bill had been very quiet. Laura realized during breakfast that he was thinking about the day ahead. For both of them, the passion story carried particular significance, though they approached it from quite different angles. Bill had grown up with the heartfelt hymns of the Wesleys, 'with what rapture gaze we on those glorious scars',[1] and a faith which related to Jesus' suffering in a deeply personal way. For him, the significance of Jesus was concentrated in his passion and death.

Laura, though familiar with this tradition, had not found it helpful. Then the whole passion story gained new meaning for her as revealing God on the side of the suffering and powerless. 'This is going to be quite a day for both of us, Bill,' she said.

The pilgrims were going to follow the last 24 hours of Jesus' life, visiting the various sites on the way to the crucifixion. 'But,' said Julia, 'we're not going to Bethany again today, although that's where the passion story really starts. Apart from Luke, all the Gospels tell us of an anointing in Bethany. Matthew and Mark describe this as happening in the house of Simon the Leper, whereas John's Gospel puts it in the home of Lazarus. We are going to start this morning in what is called the Upper Room, the place of the Last Supper. It's on Mount Zion, south-west of the old city.'

When they arrived there, Brenda couldn't hide her disappointment. It looked nothing like the Upper Room with a long table as she had imagined. Rather, it was a large empty room with a few pillars. Before Julia could give any explanation, Richard gasped, 'It's a mosque!' They were in a chapel of a twelfth-century building which had been converted into a mosque in the sixteenth century.

'This is certainly not *the* Upper Room!' Ian stated.

'No, clearly not,' Julia replied, 'but it is thought to be the site where first-century Christians gathered. So why not imagine the Last Supper to have taken place here.'

'The Last Supper – surely it was a passover meal,' said Fiona. 'Jesus and his disciples made all the traditional Jewish preparations.'

'Just a Passover meal?' Brenda was not convinced. For her, it was a meal Jesus shared with his friends, not to commemorate the Jewish past but to celebrate the Christian future. 'Surely that won't hold water historically,' said Ian. 'Jesus was a good Jew, not the first Christian!'

Richard shook his head. 'Of course Jesus was a Jew, humanly speaking, but he lived and died for all of us Christians in the future, and the Last Supper shows just that. There's a passage in 1 Corinthians where Paul tells us what Jesus said during the last supper. He clearly intended his followers to celebrate him.'

'I'm not sure you can put it like that, Richard,' Julia replied, 'but certainly Paul offers us a very old tradition about the Last Supper, older than the Gospels. In fact, the old liturgy which Paul is quoting here[2] has made it into our communion liturgy.'

'Doesn't this show how important the Last Supper was for Jesus and the first Christians?' asked Brenda.

'Important, yes,' said Julia, 'but I think it was important for Jesus in a slightly different way. He didn't encourage any worship of himself. What mattered to him was striving for God's kingdom. In the Last Supper when he celebrated the community in which he lived, he instituted a new covenant. His disciples were to re-enact this meal as a sign of this new covenant with God. It was no coincidence that he chose a meal as the sign. I think that this conveyed to them something of the essence of what he was and of how he taught God's ways. That's how he showed them the kingdom he was passionate about. So he was alive in this supper, with his loving and forgiving and challenging presence.'

They fell silent. Julia was quite reserved and it wasn't often that she spoke with such feeling and conviction about what she believed.

Bill was one of those moved. He had always associated the Last Supper much more with Jesus' death than with his life and

God's kingdom. He needed to think about that. Suddenly he made another connection. 'Wasn't it then that Jesus washed his disciples' feet?' he asked.

'Yes,' said Julia, 'it's only in John's Gospel that we find the foot-washing at that point in the passion story where the other Gospels tell us about the Last Supper. We'll talk more about it tonight.

'Let's move on now to the Mount of Olives. The Gospels tell us Jesus went there to pray at night-time.'

Ian had a strong sense of expectation as they stood on the steps of the Church of All Nations half an hour later. The church was built at the foot of the Mount of Olives, beside some very ancient olive trees. This was the traditional site of Gethsemane. The tree trunks looked wizened and gnarled. How much human misery, sadness and pain they had seen over the centuries, Ian mused.

As they stood among the trees of Gethsemane, Julia asked him to read Mark's account of Jesus foretelling Peter's denial, of his taking three of the disciples aside to watch as he prayed, and of those three falling asleep as he struggled to accept what was to come.[3]

'These scenes touch the heart of human experience,' said Julia. 'Which feels closest to you? Grappling with the future? Or coming to terms with past denial and failure?'

Ian, who had always observed the gospel from a distance with a historic interest, suddenly recognized some Gospel story in his own life. Was it this that drew people to the Christian faith?

Julia's voice interrupted his thoughts. 'You know what happens next. Judas appears with an armed crowd and identifies Jesus by greeting him with a kiss.'

'I've always wondered about this,' said Brenda. 'Did they really need Judas?'

'I guess Jesus wasn't as well known as we fondly imagine so Judas would've been helpful,' Laura answered, 'but who was it who actually arrested Jesus?'

Richard had his Bible open and said it was a crowd sent by the Jewish leaders.

Julia corrected him. 'It's interesting to note which Jewish leaders these are – namely the Temple authorities. The trouble caused by Jesus in the Temple was the most likely reason for his arrest. And in John's Gospel there is additional information indicating that the Temple police and a detachment of Roman soldiers co-operated over the arrest.'

Ian wondered aloud: 'Was that really likely?'

Fiona said she could imagine the establishment authorities co-operating over the Passover festival period to keep things quiet, and Julia agreed that that was a possibility. 'But,' she added, 'what's even more important is how Jewish and Roman leaders interacted after the arrest. Let's wander across to the supposed place of the Jewish trial.'

They walked along the Kidron valley and crossed it. A flight of very ancient steps believed to go back to the time of Jesus led them to St Peter Gallicantu, a church thought to have been built on the site of the high priest Caiaphas' house. The church was called after the cock-crow which reminded Peter of his denial of Jesus. On their way, Julia explained that it was not quite clear what actually happened to Jesus during that night. Was it a trial before the Sanhedrin (i.e. the Jewish council with the high priest as President) during the night, as Matthew and Mark would have it – although there might have been a Jewish law in force which prohibited trials at night? Or was it a less formal interrogation the following morning, as Luke describes it? Or was it an interrogation in the high priest's house, involving both Annas, an ex-high priest and his son-in-law Caiaphas, the high priest, as John tells the story?

Richard was bewildered. He looked through his Bible, and sure enough, Julia was right, there were differences in the Gospel accounts. He had never noticed this before. How could this most important of all nights in Jesus' life not be adequately recorded in the New Testament?

Below the Church of St Peter Gallicantu archaeologists had discovered an ancient prison. A chill went through Bill's bones – Jesus might have been held in that prison. As they stood together staring into the bleak space below them, Julia read a prayer for prisoners in Israel and around the world.

Use us now, Lord, as channels of your blessing for those in detention, especially any who are in particular distress at this moment.

We thank you for the courage of those who suffer for truth and freedom; and we ask, not only that they may be strengthened by our prayers, but also that we will be inspired by their example; in the love of Jesus Christ our Lord.[4]

Laura was deeply moved by these associations. It inspired her faith that Jesus was present in the pits human beings dug for each other. But it was more than simply the presence of Jesus in suffering. Seeing Jesus as a political prisoner or prisoner of conscience was important to her because it meant he wasn't just a victim but a martyr: he stood for something for which he was willing to die. That was a position of strength rather than weakness. But what did Jesus stand for? And was that the reason for his arrest and death sentence?

'This', Laura said, 'is the ultimate question. I used to think that Jesus was a kind of anarchist, opposed to Jewish law, and a revolutionary, opposed to the establishment. Now I realize that's a bit too simplistic. But I still don't think Jesus died seeing his death as Christian theology later interpreted it.'

As they were slowly walking out of the church, Ian responded typically with his historical musings. 'I can well imagine Jesus wouldn't have had in mind what he is supposed to have said when on trial. Think about it: we've got stories about two trials. So we gather *something* happened before the Temple authorities and *something* happened before Pilate. Who is supposed to have recorded what they all said? When Christians later wrote up the story of Jesus they filled in the trial dialogues in a way they thought was most natural and meaningful to them as a Christian community some decades later. We can't really know what happened or what was said.'

Julia, pointing them in the direction of the site for the trial before Pilate, didn't completely agree with this. She felt a historical-critical reading of the Gospels combined with a knowledge of the historical context was able to provide *some* sort of framework for our understanding of events. But certainly it was important to remember that the Gospels were written in the light of Easter and after the formation of a specifically Christian community. 'Think of the charge the high priest levels against Jesus in Matthew and Mark,' she continued. 'He's accused of blasphemy for calling himself the Messiah, the Son of God. This sounds more like a Christian profession of faith after Easter than a likely charge in Jesus' lifetime. On the other hand, some people accused of sorcery at the time of Jesus did get into trouble for calling themselves Sons of God, whatever that might have meant.'

'I'm not sure what other people thought of Jesus,' said Richard, 'but I'll stick with the best sources we've got – the Gospels. And whoever else called themselves Sons of God, I'm sure this is who Jesus *knew* he was. That knowledge gave him the strength to go through those trials.'

'Yes,' Bill added, 'and how much strength Jesus needed with the suffering of the crucifixion still to come.' He was only just realizing how much happened even in the lead-up to the crucifixion.

'What a man,' Laura said on cue just as they came to an ancient arch called the Ecce homo – named after Pilate's 'Here is the man' when he presented Jesus to the crowds.[5] They had arrived at the traditional site of Jesus' Roman trial before Pilate. Entering the Convent of the Sisters of Zion, they came to the Lithostrotos, the Roman pavement of the courtyard outside Pilate's headquarters, the praetorium.

Julia read to them John 18.28 according to which the Jewish leaders brought Jesus before Pilate on the following morning without entering Pilate's headquarters. At the end of the scene before Pilate, John speaks of the Lithostrotos where Pilate pronounced his judgement.[6]

This particular pavement was probably laid a couple of hundred years after Jesus. But as Ian stared at the ancient stones, it dawned on him that this was the place where Jesus' fate would have been sealed. Whatever the Jews might have wanted, capital punishment was a right the Roman empire reserved for its own authorities.

Julia explained that what took place with Jesus would have been a regular Roman trial in which the defendant got three chances to answer any accusations. Jesus' silence would have appeared to be self-condemnatory and the guilty verdict inevitable.

'I've often felt a bit sorry for Pilate, really,' said Brenda. 'I don't think he could prevent everything happening the way it did. And yet he is the only one mentioned in the creed.'

Julia responded that there was a tendency in the Gospels to shift the blame for Jesus' death away from the Romans towards the Jews. And many scholars thought that not all the stories around Pilate in the Gospels were actually historical.

While Brenda was surprised, Richard looked irritated. 'Why?' he asked. Julia pointed out that for instance the festival amnesty rule according to which Pilate offered to release Jesus rather than Barabbas, lacked support in historical evidence. 'It was probably Matthew who created the story about Pilate's wife's dream.[7] Dreams already occur in the birth story of Jesus, so you can see that it was typical for Matthew to express divine meaning in this way.' Richard stood there brooding while Ian wondered what could have persuaded Pilate to have Jesus executed.

'I suppose he might not have been terribly interested, really!' suggested Brenda. Ian countered that some of the exchanges between Jesus and Pilate were really quite deep, especially those from John's Gospel where Pilate takes Jesus inside for a chat.

'Well, Ian, you know that although John's Gospel has some really interesting historical nuggets about the passion story, we really can't say whether the conversations between Pilate and Jesus are historical,' said Julia. 'But one thing is a recurring theme, and that is the name "King of the Jews" which Pilate calls Jesus to his face and on the cross. To use this title would have sounded threatening and worrying for any occupying force, especially

before a festival. So in the end Pilate handed Jesus over for crucifixion – and did that, according to John's Gospel, on the judge's
bench on the Lithostrotos, right here.'

Ian finally got his chance to point out some carvings which he
had spotted on the pavement. They were carvings of games Roman
soldiers used to play.

'You all know what happens next, don't you?' said Julia. She
was referring to the soldiers who dressed Jesus up as a king and
mocked and abused him.

Brenda turned to Harold. 'I hate that bit,' she said, 'it's almost
worse than the crucifixion itself.'

Richard had gone quiet but as he was looking through the Gospel
stories he noticed that apart from the torture by the soldiers, not
only did Pilate have Jesus flogged but some charges of the Jewish
Council also abused Jesus before he ever got to Pilate.

'All part of the grim rhythm of brutality and oppression,' said
Laura quietly. She and Bill looked at each other and, while Laura
found the thought of ongoing brutality and oppression around the
world overwhelming, Bill was moved by the thought that this
Jesus in whom he believed suffered so much for him.

With these thoughts they set off down the Via Dolorosa to the
place of crucifixion. Julia had mentioned to them that this was
not the historic route which Jesus would have taken. But the Via
Dolorosa would lead them to the Church of the Holy Sepulchre,
the assumed site of Golgotha. Ian pointed out that the stations did
not necessarily refer to known historical incidents when Jesus
walked there.

Richard was suddenly finding things very difficult. They had
arrived at one of the most important sites for Jesus' life, and he
felt he was losing touch with the certainties of faith which he
cherished.

As the group walked the Via Dolorosa with its Stations of the
Cross, they stopped at only one station, that of Simon of Cyrene
who was forced to carry the cross for Jesus after he fell.

With challenge in his voice, Richard asked Julia whether she thought the episode of Simon was as fictitious as the other Bible stories she had 'dismantled'.

'No, no,' Julia replied. 'In fact Simon of Cyrene is really well attested historically and we assume his two sons, Alexander and Rufus, whom Mark mentions in passing, were members of the early Church. But isn't that a wonderful story of Simon carrying the cross for Jesus. Endless meditations have been written on that subject. And it's a special story for African Christians because Cyrene is in North Africa. Now think of someone for whom you carry something or of someone who carries something for you, think of people you've promised to pray for or who pray for you.'

Quietly, Brenda and Fiona sang their joint favourite song:[8]

Brother, Sister, let me serve you
let me be as Christ to you;
pray that I may have the grace to
let you be my servant, too.

They passed the Station of the Cross which commemorates Jesus meeting the Daughters of Jerusalem. Richard could not help feeling scornful at all the non-scriptural traditions that had built up around the Via Dolorosa until he realized that the episode was actually recorded by Luke. And of course later, when the disciples had fled, it was again women who at least kept a distant vigil for Jesus.

How Richard wished for Linda to be with him. She could lift his spirits.

It was a thoughtful group which continued to the Church of the Holy Sepulchre.

Bill was humming to himself one of *his* favourite hymns:

There is a green hill far away,
without a city wall,
where the dear Lord was crucified,
who died to save us all.

Suddenly, he stopped. The Church of the Holy Sepulchre, marking the site of Calvary, came into view. It was within the city walls and definitely not on a green hill far away! How could the hymn writer get it so wrong? Richard assured him that the Bible also said that the crucifixion took place outside the city walls. The explanation for this apparent contradiction turned out to be pretty simple – the city walls were extended a few decades after Jesus' death, thus incorporating this site for Golgotha.

Julia had prepared them for the scandal of the six Christian denominations who were sharing the church but not co-operating very well at the very site of Jesus' crucifixion. And sure enough, there was evidence of different Christian traditions celebrating their various services simultaneously in different parts of the building.

They stood at the supposed rock of Calvary. 'And are we sure this is the place?' asked Ian. 'Not really,' was Julia's predictable reply. 'The true location is somewhat lost in the mist of time, but this is a possible site. Golgotha means place of a skull and the rock here which resembles a skull has led people to make the associa-tion. But tomorrow, when we go to the Garden Tomb, we'll see another possible site by a rocky hill resembling a skull.'

They looked at the big rock with chapels attached. This was the place to remember the crucifixion and Bill read them the crucial verses from Mark 15.22–4.

Brenda shuddered. She had seen a film about Jesus' crucifixion and while she had not been keen at all on the graphic depiction of violence, it had made her realize to what extent those few verses compressed a lot of suffering: bringing Jesus to Golgotha, offering a drink, and crucifying him and dividing his clothes.

Fiona said that for all their cultural achievements the Romans really had a horrible way of killing people. 'Only slaves and foreigners, though!' Ian interjected. 'Well, great, that's all right then!' was Fiona's sarcastic reply. 'OK, you two,' said Julia, while Ian mumbled that he hadn't been serious. 'It certainly was a par-ticularly gruesome way of execution and it was understood to be degrading – that's why Paul speaks of *not* being ashamed of the cross of Christ, although it was such a shameful way of dying (1 Corinthians 1.23; Galatians 3.13). Even in the first century having your leader crucified was not a great way of starting a new religious movement!'

'Why was the drink offered to Jesus? Was it to comfort him or was it a spiteful act?' Laura asked. Richard said it fulfilled an Old Testament prophecy of being given vinegar to drink, and Julia added, 'Yes, that's Matthew's explanation, and he gives it a hostile spin. The other possibility is that the drink was given in order to dull the pain. But in either case Jesus does not take it.'

Laura wondered whether this was to show how strong he was. Julia nodded and said that part of the passion story in the Gospel was told in such a way as to present Jesus as a perfect model for times of persecution.

'No!' Bill said. 'You can't just make out the passion to be a story on how well Jesus behaved and that we should do likewise. Jesus suffered for us, on our behalf, to pay for our sins. That's what it's about. We can't imitate that!'

Ian retorted that they were looking at history here, at what actually happened, not how the story of Jesus had been interpreted. 'What's the point of that, then?' Fiona asked. Meanwhile, Richard and Bill thought that there could be no distinction between what had happened and what it meant since Jesus' life and death were part of God's plan to save the world.

Julia said that there was no history without interpretation, without a sense of meaningfulness in certain events of the past. It was on this basis that the Church of the Holy Sepulchre had been built, because the death of Jesus was understood to be important and more important than the death of many other prisoners. Whether Jesus' death was part of God's plan was of course a matter of interpretation.

'Of course,' she said, 'I don't think the meaning of Jesus' death can be reduced to an ethical impulse. But still, the tradition of the passion story has been shaped partly by the experience of persecution, so Christians would obviously have identified with Jesus' suffering and looked for a model in him.

'You see, there are layers of understanding, from what Jesus meant himself to how he was understood by his contemporaries and his first followers, to the understanding of the early Church and the church tradition over the centuries and finally to our understanding at the beginning of the twenty-first century. And the different life experience of these different people, Roman official, early Christian martyr and so on, throws a particular light on their understanding.'

Ian grinned and said he could see now why he with his historical interest was pursuing the question of why Jesus was killed rather more than the meaning of his death.

Meanwhile, Brenda had sat down quietly in front of one of the altars, watching pilgrims filing past. 'This is such a moving place. Look at all the love expressed here, the candles, the icons, the silver all around the altar. Jesus' death means so much!'

For a moment, they fell silent.

Bill stared at the altar. The Church of the Holy Sepulchre was beautifully adorned and he had expected it to be the highlight of his pilgrimage. But he could not relate to this place, the very place of Jesus' death. Somehow, the dungeon at St Peter Gallicantu had impressed him more than this. He had always understood Jesus' death as the culmination of his life. Now, it did not seem to make sense.

Richard had also been looking at the altar. 'Really,' he said, 'I know all these beautiful things are well-meant, but isn't all this a huge distraction from his horrific death on the cross?'

'I can see what you mean, Richard,' said Julia. 'I guess it's not my thing to dwell on the ins and outs of Jesus' crucifixion. That's something I share with people in antiquity who thought it was so awful that there are very few descriptions of crucifixions. But you're right, we need to remember that by all accounts Jesus was nailed hands and feet to the cross and in that painful and helpless position he was jeered and mocked by passers-by, and even by those crucified beside him. It doesn't bear thinking about.'

Fiona asked Bill what actually caused death in crucifixion. She knew he'd read up about it. Apparently, after a slow and painful period of time, it was mainly asphyxiation which caused death. Breaking the legs of a crucified person, therefore, was an act of mercy in that it hastened death. But Jesus had died before the Roman soldiers came round to doing this.

'How easy it is to forget what's involved when we wear a cross around our neck . . .' murmured Fiona. 'Yes, or see the cross on an altar in church,' added Laura.

Everyone looked somewhat chastened; they felt it was all too easy to sanitize the thought of Jesus' death. Julia invited them to take some time out in the church, to wander to the various places where Jesus' death was remembered. As she gave them a sheet with some of the last words of Jesus to meditate on, she hummed the words of one of those crucified beside Jesus: Jesus, remember me, when you come into your kingdom.

Matthew's Gospel and Mark's Gospel

'My God, my God, why have you forsaken me?' (Matthew 27.46 and Mark 15.24)

Jesus dies with a loud cry and the curtain of the Temple is torn in two.

Matthew also records an earthquake and people rising from the dead.

Reaction of the centurion: This man was God's son.

Luke's Gospel

'Father, into your hands I commend my spirit.' (Luke 23.46)

With this, he dies.

Reaction of the centurion: This man was innocent.

John's Gospel

Jesus refers his mother and favoured disciple to each other.
  'I am thirsty.' (John 19.28)
  After receiving wine he says, 'It is finished.' (John 19.30)

Laura was once again struck by the desolation of the cry in Matthew's and Mark's Gospels, a cry she heard reverberating around the world to this day. She hummed Julia's tune and thought of Jesus' forgiveness of his torturers and his promise to the criminal crucified beside him that he would be in Paradise with him the same day. When she realized she could not see those verses on her sheet, she asked Julia about it. It turned out that this passage was peculiar to Luke's Gospel and was followed by Jesus' commending his spirit.

Meanwhile, Brenda meditated on the scene of mother and disciple in John's Gospel. It spoke to her of Jesus' life culminating in love.

A little later, Bill was especially keen to raise with Julia Matthew's and Mark's reference to the Temple. 'Isn't this the sign that in his death Jesus is opening the way to God for all?' he asked.

Richard, who was still taking in the differences in the Gospel stories about Jesus' death, feared what Julia might say. As he expected, Julia thought the story of the curtain of the Temple tearing was legendary and part of the interpretation of Jesus' death. 'You see,' she said 'the Temple is one of the Jewish reference points which the Gospel writers make. Jesus' last words are largely inspired by psalms. The tearing of the curtain shows how Jesus continues to be on collision course with the Jewish Temple aristocracy. It's a foretaste of the Temple's destruction. You can also see it as an indication that Jesus is the new atoning sacrifice, replacing the Temple.'

'Did he make a sacrifice or was he sacrificed?' Fiona asked. 'I find that idea of Jesus and sacrifice repulsive – either, if he made a sacrifice, he was on a religiously motivated suicide mission, or, if he was sacrificed, he was a player in a gruesome drama directed by God. And I wouldn't want any part in that!'

She was whispering with such agitation that Julia had to quieten her down. 'It's open to debate whether Jesus himself understood his death as sacrificial, but certainly his Jewish followers did. They experienced reconciliation with God through Jesus and in their minds reconciliation comes about in terms of sacrifice. There is also the link to Passover, suggesting that Jesus is the Passover lamb. But seeing Jesus as a sacrifice changes the idea of sacrifice. Certainly in the Apostle Paul's understanding, preceding the Gospels, this sacrifice is somehow offered by God and it is not about changing God but about changing ourselves. In that sense there is also continuity with Jesus' life because he called people to change.'

Bill suddenly realized that the passion really only made sense to him if he linked it with what Jesus was passionate about. Jesus had offered himself to follow God's will to death, and for this he had Bill's undying devotion. But that will of God was also expounded in Jesus' ministry on earth. And somehow there was a connection between, on the one side, Jesus' passion and death sentence and, on the other, Jesus' passionate message, his interpretation of the law, his critique of the Temple, his preaching of the kingdom and its messianic overtones picked up by his followers. Jesus' ministry was provocative and in the end it led to total rejection when even his disciples fled and the women were left standing and watching from a distance.

On his walk around the church, Ian had spotted the tomb of Christ. He asked Julia what would have customarily happened to the body of a crucified person. She answered that usually burial would not have been allowed for a crucified man. But in Jesus' case Joseph of Arimathea, whom John's Gospel names in the same breath as Nicodemus as a sympathetic Jew of some standing, takes the body hastily before the sabbath and buries it in his own tomb – an entombment rather than a burial and an endorsement of Jesus by a leading Jew.

More questions than answers were flying around the little group as they left the Church of the Holy Sepulchre. It struck Brenda as strange that there was no time for a funeral rite.

'Ah,' said Laura, 'but what about the women coming with spices?' Julia explained that the sabbath had interrupted the usual burial customs. 'The women who came to the tomb wanting to anoint Jesus are part of the Easter story. But before we go, let's use the opportunity in this place which marks Jesus' death, to remember and give thanks for people we love who have gone before us. After a moment of silence I'll say the Kontakion:'

Give rest, O Christ, to your servant with the saints:
where sorrow and pain are no more,
neither sighing, but life everlasting.
You only are immortal, the creator and maker of all:
and we are mortal, formed from the dust of the earth,
And unto earth shall we return.
For so you ordained when you created me, saying:
'Dust you are and to dust you shall return.'
All of us go down to the dust,
yet weeping at the grave, we make our song:
Alleluia! Alleluia! Alleluia!
Give rest, O Christ, to your servant with the saints:
where sorrow and pain are no more,
neither sighing, but life everlasting.

* * *

The evening meeting, it was clear, would have a full agenda.

'It's been rather a full day,' said Julia, 'in more ways than one. And of course there is a lot to follow up. So let me simply present some of the background to the issues that we touched on during the day.'

1. The Last Supper

The words of institution are very similar in the synoptic Gospels which present the Last Supper as a Passover meal. Compare Matthew 26.26–9; Mark 14.22–5; Luke 22.14–20. Only Luke mentions two cups whereas the others have one cup. A Passover meal is thought to have four cups, and none of the Gospels give any details on the meal and its symbolic elements. Hence it is hotly debated whether the Last Supper was actually a Passover meal or not.

The oldest account of the words of institution can be found in Paul's First Letter to the Corinthians 11.23–6.

The synoptic Gospels say that the Passover began at sunset on the day we call Thursday. John's Gospel dates the Passover differently. He agrees with the other Gospels that Jesus was crucified on the afternoon of the day we call Friday, but says that this was at the time when the lambs were being killed in preparation for the Passover (John 19.14, 42), which began at sunset. Thus John presents Jesus as the true Passover lamb, but the Last Supper with the Twelve (John 13.21–30) is not a Passover meal.

However, John uses that meal to discuss how the betrayer is one of the disciples who has table fellowship with Jesus. Preceding this, John's Gospel presents a story which is a theological parallel to the Last Supper in the synoptic Gospels. It is the story of the foot-washing. Like table fellowship, it is another symbol of community life, but with a particularly challenging edge to it. Jesus teaches service to one another – we might talk today of 'servant leadership'.

Nonetheless, there is eucharistic theology in John's Gospel as well. In the context of the Feeding of the Five Thousand in John 6, Jesus presents himself as the Bread of Life.

2. Historical factors leading to Jesus' death

Different factors conspired to lead to Jesus' crucifixion and we thought about some of them yesterday.

The ruling classes in Jerusalem, the Temple aristocracy and the Romans, saw a potential cause of serious unrest in Jesus and would have wanted to silence him. His preaching of the kingdom and his interpretation of the Torah and of what was of value within the Jewish faith had the potential to threaten the Roman and Jewish Temple establishment. Jesus appears both uninterested in and un-afraid of the Romans and shows prophetic anger vis-à-vis the Temple.

Jewish crowds called for Jesus' death. While we may assume that the crowds welcoming Jesus upon his entry to Jerusalem were country people who had travelled to Jerusalem for the festival, it is likely that the bloodthirsty mob were city people.

To what extent Jesus foresaw or even provoked his death is an open question. He must have realized the danger of going to Jerusalem. There is an interesting note in Luke 13.31 in which the Pharisees – for once shown in a positive light – warn Jesus of Herod. Jesus' response is prophetic indeed: he affirms that it is unthinkable for a prophet to meet his death anywhere but in Jerusalem.

3. Models for understanding Jesus' death

In the New Testament, the synoptic Gospels, the Pauline epistles, the Johannine literature and the Letter to the Hebrews offer us varied theological perspectives. Each of them has a developed understanding of the death of Jesus but we cannot explore this here in any detail. It is interesting as well as sad that later developments of Christian doctrine through the centuries to this present day, both denominationally and across the denominations, have produced barely reconcilable differences between Christians.

All I want to do now is point to four basic models for understanding Jesus' death.

(a) Passover and sacrifice

The concept of sacrifice is more implied than explicit in the Gospels. We talked about this earlier today. In the Last Supper – whether it was a Passover meal or not – Jesus instituted a new covenant. The whole context of the Passover festival suggests a sacrificial understanding, with Jesus as the new Passover lamb replacing the rituals taking place at the Temple. The Letter to the Hebrews emphasizes this sacrificial and liturgical theme (Hebrews 10). It is unclear to what extent Jesus reckoned with his death, understood it as sacrificial, or indeed saw any particular theological meaning in it. It may well be that Jesus saw himself as the suffering righteous one of Israel's prophetic tradition and as a martyr who had to sacrifice his life for God's cause and for the benefit of his people. Certainly, one of the most striking features of his foretelling of his suffering and death is the divine 'must' in the sense of 'all this must happen (Mark 8.31–3 and parallels) because God has predetermined it'. On the other hand, some scholars argue that any such understanding of Jesus' foreknowledge or intentions stems from the disciples' post-Easter faith rather than from Jesus himself.

Let me add a word on the idea of sacrifice. Reconciliation with God lies at the heart of the sacrifice. Paul says that God has reconciled us to himself through Christ (2 Corinthians 5.18). The important point here is that it is not God needing to be reconciled with us but us with God. Nevertheless, it is God who offers sacrifice through Jesus rather than humankind offering sacrifice to God. So not only is the Temple sacrifice replaced – a possible explanation of the tearing of the curtain – but the whole idea of sacrifice is transformed.

(b) Ransom

Another very powerful way of understanding Jesus' death is in terms of a ransom (Mark 10.45; Matthew 20.28: 'The Son of Man came . . . to give his life a ransom for many'). The idea of Jesus buying with his own life and thus liberating the faithful, just as slaves might be bought and set free, is further developed in Paul's theology and became an influential concept in Christian thought. Historically speaking, I don't think this is an understanding worked out in the mind of Jesus and his disciples – certainly not in the sense of a liberation either from our individual wrongdoings or from original sin. But the seed for Paul's interpretation might have been in Jesus' mind, that is, seeing a redemptive quality in his death, buying and setting Israel free by drawing on himself the judgement he proclaimed for his people.

In the saying about the ransom, it is not clear who it is that demands or receives the ransom. Rather, the dominant idea is of Jesus giving himself *voluntarily*. If you look at the context of Jesus' 'ransom' saying, you find him talking about an ethos of radical service which characterizes his own life and should characterize the life of his disciples. To speak of Jesus 'giving his life a ransom for many' emphasizes starkly that his central purpose was to serve and not to be served.

(c) Glorification

In John's Gospel, Jesus appears serene and divine, a king from another realm. The beginning of the passion story signals his departure from this world (John 13.1). His death on the cross is understood as an elevation, a paradoxical glorification which shows the way to the Father (John 3.14; 12.23–6). Death, resurrection and ascension are all part of the 'lifting up' process of the Son of Man which may have its roots in the Suffering Servant sayings from the Book of Isaiah, such as 52.13.

(d) Identification with suffering

God's identification with human suffering has been a fruitful concept in twentieth-century theology. In the Gospels we find its roots in the persecuted early Christians' identification with Jesus. The apocalyptic passages of the Gospels give us a clue here when they speak of Jesus' followers having to stand before governors and kings – just like Jesus in the passion story.

There are two related motifs here: one is the exemplary role of Jesus, as in his prayerfulness in Gethsemane, his willingness to yield to God's will, his repudiation of violence. The other is the recognition of Christ's presence in those who are suffering. This idea is an extension of the parable of the Judgement of the Nations from Matthew's Gospel (Matthew 25.31–46), where the original emphasis lies on the call to help the poor rather than on a theological statement about God's bias for and special presence with the poor.

And all this is about suffering. But of course Jesus' death has also inspired Christians to trust that even in death they are not in a place remote from him. It is really important to see that the motivating force behind all the four models is love: Jesus would have sacrificed or given his life as a ransom out of love. God so loved the world that he gave his only Son, and God shows his love for those who are persecuted and suffering.

I often think the only response to all of this is silent and prayerful awe before the mystery that is the passion of Jesus Christ. So let us keep silent for a moment and offer into the presence of Christ our hurts and sufferings and the sufferings of those whom we know.

Then I shall say a collect for Good Friday:[9]

Eternal God,
in the cross of Jesus
we see the cost of our sin
and the depth of your love:

in humble hope and fear
may we place at his feet
all that we have and all that we are,
through Jesus Christ our Lord.

And everyone said 'Amen'.

Questions for discussion

1. Richard is worried by questions about the historicity of some events in the Gospel accounts of the last days of Jesus. How would you try to reassure him?

2. What does the Last Supper (Holy Communion, Eucharist, Mass) mean to you and how do you relate to Jesus through it?

3. How do you react to the tradition in which Bill was brought up (the significance of Jesus was concentrated in his passion and death)?

4. Which of the four interpretations of the death of Jesus do you find most helpful? Try to explain why.

5. What does Jesus' suffering and death mean to you for your own suffering and death?

11

The Resurrection

'The last day of the pilgrimage for the first day of the week!' Julia announced as they set off early on the final day. She asked Brenda to read to them the second verse of chapter 16 of Mark's Gospel: 'Very early on the first day of the week, when the sun had risen, they went to the tomb.'

Amid the murmur of recognition of the beginning of the Easter Gospel, Fiona looked over Brenda's shoulder to see who 'they' were. 'It's the three women,' said Brenda, 'Mary Magdalene, Mary the mother of James and Salome.' Julia added that they were the counterparts of Peter, James and John, the three disciples Jesus had with him at earlier key points of his life, at the transfiguration and in the Garden of Gethsemane.

'It's another sign of love, isn't it,' said Brenda, 'that the women want to anoint Jesus.' It reminded Fiona of Jesus' anointing by the anonymous woman in preparation for his burial. The anointing formed a ritual frame around the story of the passion, said Julia.

The pilgrims were on their way to the Garden Tomb. In the nineteenth century, an Englishman had identified a place north of Damascus Gate as the possible site for the crucifixion. It was a rocky hill which he thought looked like a human skull, and it had a first-century tomb nearby. Thanks to an English charity, the area around the rock was made into a beautiful garden, a quiet place of retreat.

They looked at the sizeable tomb, big enough to walk around in, and realized that if its entrance had been barred by one huge stone, it would have been a heavy stone indeed, too heavy to shift.

When they sat down under the trees in the garden, Ian asked Julia whether she really believed in the resurrection. After all, Mark, the earliest Gospel, did not really have an Easter story. The women just fled in terror from an empty tomb.

'There's nothing like getting the big questions out of the way first!' Julia smiled. 'I don't quite know where to start. First of all,

Mark's account isn't the earliest reference to Easter. Paul, in his First Letter to the Corinthians, chapter 15, recounts an apostolic tradition of appearances of the risen Jesus to Peter, the Twelve and five hundred believers, James and all the apostles. We think Paul heard of this early on in his ministry, so about forty years before Mark's Gospel.

'Do I believe in the resurrection? Well, of course it depends what you mean by that. Ideas put forward against the resurrection include that Jesus didn't die in the first place, that the disciples suffered mass hallucination or that Jesus rose in the hearts of the believers who kept him alive by keeping his message alive. None of these cut much ice with me.'

Ian interrupted: 'But all these are arguments people developed later against Easter faith. What did resurrection actually mean in the first century? Was it about the everlasting soul?'

Laura said that their vicar always emphasized that it was a bodily resurrection and that the risen Jesus wasn't just a spirit. It was important to her that physical body as part of the material world was honoured and did not become a disposable item. 'You know,' she said, 'immortality of the soul also makes life after death sound as natural a function as waking after sleep. Surely death's a bit more serious than that.'

'You're right,' Julia responded. 'Easter is definitely not about the immortality of the soul. That's a concept alien to Jesus' world, and therefore it is vital to understand what resurrection meant in first-century Jewish thought. It is not a general term for life after death but is related to God's justice – God justifying God's people. At a time of great suffering and martyrdom, for example, the conviction grew that God does not forsake the holy fools and martyrs who are crushed under the wheels of this world. As a result, the Maccabean martyrs, those Jewish freedom fighters, rejoiced in the hope of receiving their bodies back intact after death, and the Pharisees believed in the resurrection of the body. Consequently, the resurrection stories stress bodily continuity – Jesus shows the marks on his hands and feet, is hungry and eats – and Easter is seen as God's protest against injustice, darkness and death.

Richard listened with interest but was impatient. 'So do *you* believe in the resurrection?' he asked.

Julia responded that she would answer his question but really wanted to know what they believed, what they associated with Easter and what it meant to them.

Unexpectedly, Harold chipped in. He had been very quiet for the last day or two. Drawing meaning from the suffering of Jesus was something he always found difficult and even contrived. But the positive sense of Easter appealed to him because it gave people hope and comfort. 'Yes, it does,' said Laura, looking around. 'Just look at all the people in this place, praying or sharing communion. And that's fine. But surely, the Easter message has more to say than that. Isn't there also something quite challenging about God being on the side of the downtrodden? The Easter story tells me that compliance and collusion with the established powers of the world isn't God's way. Just think of the huge wall dividing the two communities here in Jerusalem, isolating especially the Palestinians. Then think of the huge stone that needed to be rolled away in front of Jesus' tomb. Isn't Easter all about overcoming death and death-dealing ways?'

Brenda smiled. She was so enjoying the beautiful layout of the garden and its flowers. What Laura said was a bit heavy for her. 'I love that Easter story when Mary Magdalene thinks Jesus is the gardener. Do you remember Cat Stevens singing "Morning has broken"? "Morning has broken like the first morning" – that's what I imagine it to have been like, a bit like the first day of creation in the Garden of Eden. And like this wonderful garden around us, it's a sign of God's love for us. God loves us and gives us life. I think that's why Jesus was raised again, to be our loving friend always. Does that sound all right, Julia?'

Fiona was about to say that Brenda didn't have to ask Julia's permission for what she believed but it was time for them to move on.

Bill was deeply moved. Actually, he mused, the resurrection was at least as important as the passion story. Jesus alive, new life: without Easter nothing made sense. It felt like a dark cloud lifting. Jesus lived on in what he was really passionate about.

On their way to Emmaus Julia explained that there were four possible sites. 'We're going to Abu Gosh, where there is a church and we'll celebrate Holy Communion there.'

Inside the Crusaders' Church at Abu Gosh, before the service, Ian read the Emmaus story from Luke 24.13–35.

'This is it,' Fiona said. 'You were asking about our understanding of the resurrection faith, Julia. Well, I think this story hands it to us on a platter. The way I see it, you have Christians with Easter faith on the one hand and you have Easter appearance stories on the other hand. And I think Easter faith came first, some sort of unexpected and mysterious experience of the risen Jesus, such as the Emmaus disciples had. From that the whole Easter story with the tomb and the appearances was developed. And yes, I do believe in Jesus' resurrection if that means we can meet him in unexpected places. But I don't believe in a bodily resurrection.'

Richard was indignant. 'Actually, Fiona, the Emmaus story tells us just the opposite. The disciples on the Emmaus road were disheartened. They learnt faith only through the presence of the risen Lord who first taught them some Gospel basics about his death before revealing himself to them at the table.'

When Fiona asked him whether he believed in the bodily resurrection Richard said that yes, of course he did, it was central to the Christian faith. 'Well,' said Fiona, 'but how does this body exist? In the various Easter stories we hear of the risen Jesus coming through doors, vanishing suddenly, and quite often simply not being recognized. That's not a human body as we know it!'

'But there are still the scars, Fiona, isn't that very human?' said Brenda hopefully.

'So?' That was Ian. He questioned the credibility of the biblical accounts anyway, because he could not imagine anything as unscientific as the resurrection actually happening. So any mention of scars just made him more suspicious, thinking that this was a feature inserted into the story to show both the authenticity and identity of Jesus' body.

But for Richard, nothing less than a bodily resurrection would do. 'It's the basis for our faith and you're going to get into an awful mess if you start picking and choosing. Paul says we are the most to be pitied if we do not believe in the resurrection. And I know in my heart that Jesus is alive!' He spoke with some defiance.

The atmosphere was still a little heated when it came to the communion service. Julia pointed out that the Emmaus story, however you wanted to interpret it historically, conveyed a deep meaning of where the risen Jesus could be met, namely in unexpected places, when feelings were low, and in fellowship with others.

'This will be our last communion service on this pilgrimage. Sharing our different approaches to faith and Jesus has been hard at times, but I hope it has enriched you, led you to develop your thinking and clarify for yourself what it is you think and believe. One lovely aspect of the Emmaus story is that the risen Jesus clearly does not demand a certain level of understanding before his presence is experienced. He's just with them when they break bread together.'

And so they broke bread together and were blessed.

'Where to now?' asked Brenda. 'Another Easter story?'

'And when are you going to say something, Julia, about what you believe?' This was Richard.

'All right,' said Julia. 'We're now on our way to the last station of our pilgrimage. It's the site of the ascension of Jesus. So we're returning to Jerusalem and going to the top of the Mount of Olives to the Chapel of the Ascension.

'Now about my understanding of Jesus' resurrection: You've all mentioned some of the very important elements of Easter faith, the revelation of God's love, the creativeness of God who brings life out of death, the ethical impulse that comes from the defeat of death and evil powers, the hope and the comfort. And when we come to the Ascension Chapel there's the aspect of Jesus reigning and being Lord of all. Luke, by the way, is the only Gospel writer who gives us the ascension story. It's as though he wants to put a full stop to the various post-Easter appearances of Jesus.'

When they arrived at the chapel they were almost deafened by the sound of birds twittering away noisily in the cupola. They stood around a giant concrete imprint of Jesus' foot which he was said to have made when he ascended. It made everyone smile; Jesus had clearly had very large feet! Julia asked Fiona to read the Ascension story not from the very end of Luke's Gospel but from the beginning of the Book of Acts.

Then together, they said an Ascension Day Collect.

Risen Christ,
you have raised our human nature to the throne of heaven:
help us to seek and serve you,
that we may join you at the Father's side,
where you reign with the Spirit in glory,
now and for ever.[1]

Laura was disappointed with the prayer. For her, the most important message of the heavenly heralds was their telling the disciples not to stand looking up toward heaven.

'This is what it's about for me,' she said. 'We're not to be so heavenly-minded that we're no earthly use; we've got to do Jesus' work here on earth. This collect seems to want to reverse things again. It makes Jesus in heaven the centre of attention rather than his message!'

'But you can't separate the two!' Richard called. Ian didn't agree. 'Just look at the proclamation of Jesus in the Gospels and then look at what the New Testament letter writers say – what's happened to the message of the kingdom? It has vanished and been replaced by a mythical Christ figure – thanks to Paul.'

'No, no,' Richard protested. 'Jesus said he is the way and the truth and the life, so of course he embodies the message.'

Ian retorted, 'Yes, and you're having to resort to the much later and theologically more reflected Gospel of John to argue this point – you could hardly do it with Mark's Gospel.'

Richard's response was prompt. 'Of course I could, just think of Jesus asking Peter at Banyas who people thought he was, just think of the transfiguration story, just think of Jesus speaking about his suffering, just think of the whole passion story! You can't take the Bible apart, it all belongs together.'

'OK, you two,' Julia interrupted them. 'Richard is right in that the New Testament as a canonical text wants to be understood as a whole and not as a quarry containing a collection of unrelated texts. There is a scholarly name for the approach which looks at the Bible as a whole called "canonical criticism". Nevertheless, analysing the constituent parts can also give us a better understanding of the whole. And I do think there is a distinct shift in emphasis between the gospel message and the epistle message. That is why I have brought you here at the end of our pilgrimage, to the place where we remember the end of Jesus' earthly life and ministry.'

'I still want to know', said Richard, 'whether you think, Julia, that we could have taken a photograph of Easter morning and of Ascension Day.' 'Well, we could have, but I don't know what we would have seen. You know that the traditional question in this regard is whether one thinks the resurrection is historical. My answer to that is "yes" and "no". No, it wasn't, in the sense of being a potentially repeatable event, something conforming to our understanding of what may happen in the course of life and history. Yes, in the sense that something certainly occurred which transformed the disciples' mission and changed the course of (church) history: Jesus, the messenger, becomes the message.

I always like to say that the empty tomb is neither a happy end nor a photo finish but the beginning of the story God writes in our lives. And that's what's written in your heart, for instance, Richard – I can see it when you tell me that you know Jesus is alive. The New Testament will enhance your understanding of that as it has nourished those who inspired *you* with the Christian faith. For I'm sure that in the first instance you believed in Jesus not because you read in the New Testament about his resurrection but because you met a community of believers whose life and faith and way of being spoke to you at a deep level, a level far deeper than that of any issue of historical reality 2,000 years ago.'

Richard felt dazed. Julia was moving the debate between them away from history to personal faith. Of course, that was what was most important to him. But was she saying that the certainties he felt to be necessary for a firm faith were elusive?

* * *

For the last time, they gathered in their meeting room in the evening. Julia had brought an Easter candle from church and placed it in the centre.

'Easter', she said, 'is the most defining element of the Jesus story. If you live and move in Christian circles all the time, it can be hard to imagine just how striking this is, that someone should rise from the dead. And without Easter, we would not be here as a group of Christian pilgrims. Without Easter, the world might remember Jesus as a footnote in history, a Jewish teacher who sought to reform the Jewish faith, one of those who along with the Pharisees paved the way for the post-Temple Jewish community which met and worshipped in synagogues. But in the light of Easter, things are different. The sharing of the Easter story marked the beginning of a religious group with an identity separate from Judaism. Initially, this beginning was blurred by the fact that all Christians were Jews, but as soon as Gentiles became converts to Jesus, a crisis was looming in the young movement which came to a head with the Apostle Paul's Gentile mission. About twenty years after Jesus' earthly life, the Jerusalem Council vindicated Paul and decided that Gentiles did not have to become Jews before becoming Christians. A community of faith distinct from Judaism had emerged.

'So much for a quick sketch of post-Easter history!

'But, you might ask, what did Jesus himself believe about the resurrection? Jesus' teaching of the kingdom implied a belief in the resurrection of all. This belief in a corporate resurrection was shared with the Pharisees. If Jesus thought of himself as rising from the dead I don't imagine him seeing this as a single and separate event. The verses in the Gospels where he does appear to predict this, are to my mind post-Easter interpretations by the early Christians.

'What I'd like to look at with you now are two important elements of the Easter story, namely the empty tomb and the appearances of the risen Jesus to his followers.'

The empty tomb

The story of the empty tomb is a solid part of the Easter story and deeply rooted in it. While its elements include women discovering the empty tomb, angelic messengers announcing Jesus' resurrection and the disciples checking up on the women's story of discovery, the details of who the women or the disciples were and how many angels were involved vary in the Gospel accounts.

The empty tomb story has given rise to all sorts of speculations, the earliest of which is noted in Matthew's Gospel. Here it is said to have been put about by the Roman soldiers that the disciples stole the body of Jesus (Matthew 28.11–15). There must have also been a suggestion that the women went to the wrong tomb. That's why you'll read in the Gospels how the women saw precisely where Jesus' body was laid.

How important is the tradition of the empty tomb for the Christian faith? Christians have given various answers to this question. For some, the empty tomb is crucial because it signifies that something happened to the dead body of Jesus. The empty tomb as a mark of the resurrection of the body shows a continuity between the earthly and risen Jesus, as do the scars shown to doubting Thomas in John's Gospel. But there are other Christians for whom the empty tomb is not important. They are concerned not to get caught up in metaphysical speculation about the way Jesus' dead body might have been transformed, and they point to the

Apostle Paul's notable silence on the empty tomb. It's certainly interesting how Paul lists his vision of the risen Christ alongside the Easter appearances to the disciples.

The experience of Jesus being alive is at the heart of the Easter message. I think stories of an empty tomb and angelic messengers are ways to communicate this truth rather than to indicate what precisely happened to Jesus' body.

The appearance stories

This leads us on to the appearances of Jesus after the resurrection. The earliest mention of them is in Paul's First Letter to the Corinthians, where Paul lists the witnesses to whom the risen Lord appeared (1 Corinthians 15.3–8). The Gospels give us more detailed appearance stories. Each has at its core the words of the risen Lord. These invariably provide an important impulse for the future of the Christian community.

In Matthew's Gospel, Jesus appears once to the women and once to the disciples.

Mark's Gospel ends abruptly with the women fleeing from the empty tomb, afraid to speak to anyone (Mark 16.1–8). It is virtually certain that Mark 16.9–20 is not part of the original Gospel but a later addition to round it off in harmony with the other Gospels. Much ink has been spent on trying to work out whether a proper ending to Mark's Gospel with Easter appearances has been lost or whether the absence of a full-blown Easter story is part of the meaning of Mark's Easter Gospel – possibly in the sense of the angel speaking of the elusiveness of the risen Jesus when he says 'he is not here, he is going ahead of you'. I find it an impossible conundrum!

Luke and John offer a variety of appearance stories. The Emmaus story in Luke is one of two appearance stories in which the risen Jesus teaches from the Scriptures. The lakeside stories in Luke and John are reminiscent of episodes in Jesus' earthly life.

The overriding message of the risen Lord is one of mission. Initially, the women at the tomb are commanded to tell the disciples of the resurrection, then the disciples are commanded to make more disciples, to teach and to baptize. The classic formulation at the end of Matthew's Gospel is accompanied by the assurance of the abiding presence of Jesus (Matthew 28.16–20). Unique to John's Gospel is the giving of the Spirit (John 20.19–23). This is John's version of the Pentecost story which Luke presents in his Book of Acts.

The nature of the physicality of the risen Lord is certainly also addressed in those appearance stories. This is the case implicitly when Jesus is not recognized, when he appears through locked doors and when he vanishes from sight. But the matter is also addressed explicitly in Luke's and John's Gospel. Jesus is touchable and needs food, so he is not a ghost or merely spiritual being, and the scars on his hands and feet indicate the continuity with the man who walked the roads of Palestine and was crucified. Those scars also show us that there is a place for wounded people with God. All this indicates to me that the whole of Jesus' life is part of the gospel to us, not just his cross and resurrection.

Sometimes the very material descriptions of the risen Jesus in the Gospels are contrasted with Paul's explanation of life after the resurrection in 1 Corinthians 15.35–57, where he speaks of a spiritual body. But I think Paul is addressing a different question here. While the risen Jesus can be seen as the forerunner, his post-Easter appearances are unique to him, before the resurrection of all at the end of time.

Basically, I believe the Easter appearance stories want to tell us something of both the reality and the mystery of the presence of the risen Lord. This presence bowled over the first disciples and this has been the experience of Christians through the centuries. The Gospels give us a yardstick for the experience by rooting it firmly in the life and teaching of Jesus.

116

Death, resurrection and ascension

Much of what can be said about the meaning of Jesus' death only makes sense in the light of his resurrection and vice versa. In fact, it is usually not at all helpful to pin a particular meaning solely on Jesus' crucifixion or on his resurrection. The revelation of God's love, the creativeness of God who brings life out of death, the defeat of death and of the evil powers that brought about Jesus' death, the understanding of Jesus as a sacrifice or ransom, his glorification, his identification with those who suffer – all these need to be connected with the events both of Holy Week and Easter. It is only in the light of the resurrection, when we see Jesus vindicated and God's love and life stronger than anything else, that everything falls into place.

To my mind, this is carried through further in the ascension, which is unique to Luke as a story. John's Gospel refers to it both implicitly in his reference to Jesus being lifted up and in the resurrection story when Jesus speaks to Mary of his ascension (John 20.17). The story of the ascension powerfully rounds off several messages about Jesus:

- it explains the end of resurrection appearances and marks the beginning of Jesus' physical absence, while also preparing for Pentecost, the sending of the Holy Spirit;
- it relates Jesus to Moses, Elijah and Enoch: according to Jewish tradition, Moses ascended; and both Elijah and Enoch were taken up into heaven by God (2 Kings 2.11; Genesis 5.24);
- it concludes the forty days after the resurrection which, like other periods involving forty in the Bible, provide a time of preparation for some new or fuller expression of divine intent;
- it indicates Jesus' defeat of powers of evil and death and his enthronement as King (Psalm 110, a coronation psalm, became important to the early Christians);
- it marks the inauguration of the kingdom and reveals Jesus' way from death to life eternal;

- and it makes a clear statement about Jesus' divinity.

In short, I believe that the ascension story relies on the world view of antiquity, with God's realm of heaven being literally above, to convey, in picture language but very powerfully, the faith and experience of the first Christians.

I know this way of looking at the ascension is a difficult one for some of you. But I don't think we can build our faith on supposed certainties of historical events. In my experience, when we want to cling to our faith it either hardens to become something rather indigestible or it slinks away. We always need to let go of our faith and receive it afresh as a gift. I have to come back to those birds in the cupola of the Chapel of the Ascension. The poet Tagore said: Faith is the bird which sings while the night is still dark.

Paul speaks of only seeing in a mirror, dimly, and we certainly fall short both in our understanding and in our living of the way of Christ.

I have lit this Easter candle which we use in baptism services because, in Christian understanding, baptism makes us part of Jesus' resurrection story. Through baptism, we share in his resurrection. Jesus could have put it differently. He would have spoken, I think, of the life of the kingdom of which we become part through baptism. Living this resurrection life, this life of the kingdom, is both a gift and a challenge. And I hope something of both will travel back home with you.

Let's offer to God a prayer of thanks for the people who have been hospitable to us. Let us pray especially for the Palestinian Christian community which at the moment is living those resurrection stories in a most unfortunate way behind locked doors for fear of the Jews. Let us pray for God's kingdom of mercy, truth and love, of justice and reconciliation to bless this land and all its peoples.

We conclude with an Easter collect:[2]

God of glory,
by the raising of your Son
you have broken the chains of death and hell:
fill your Church with faith and hope;
for a new day has dawned
and the way to life stands open
in our Saviour Jesus Christ.
Amen. Amen.

Questions for discussion

1. How important is the empty tomb to you? Why?

2. What does the resurrection of Jesus mean for your understanding of your own mortality?

3. Julia lists six points about the ascension. What do you make of them?

4. In the evening discussion on the ascension story, Julia says, 'We always need to let go of our faith and receive it afresh as a gift.' What do you think she meant by this?

12

A Transforming Experience

They were all sitting in the departure lounge of Ben Gurion airport, waiting for the flight back home.

Brenda told Harold and Fiona what a great time she'd had and thanked them for coming with her. 'I feel exhausted, elated, inspired and challenged. And I've learnt so much. I think that now, when I arrange the church flowers, I'll always think of the flowers at the Garden Tomb.' She fumbled in her handbag and her diary revealed that indeed she was on flower duty for next Sunday – and Fiona would be staffing the Fair Trade stall after church. When Julia saw that they were checking church rotas, she laughed. 'You're not wasting much time, are you, in getting back to your old routines? But here are some last questions for all of you before slotting back into life back home: *What has this pilgrimage done for you? Has it changed your view of Jesus? Has it changed anything else for you?* When we meet in a fortnight's time in Farnley, it would be good to share not just photos but also some answers to these questions.'

When they met in Farnley and looked at each other's photos, it was a chilly evening. 'And that's not the only difference from our time together in the Middle East,' Fiona observed. 'We've all, I think, been quickly absorbed again into home and church life. But we haven't forgotten about your questions, Julia, and to thank you for leading the pilgrimage, I'm presenting you with this little booklet from all of us. We gave ourselves a page each to write answers to your questions and to insert a photo of what was, for us, a key place on the pilgrimage. As the only one to have seen all the pages, I've put them into a slideshow for us to watch together now.'

They all clapped and settled down to watch together.

Brenda's page

You won't be surprised to find a picture of the Garden Tomb on my page. Though a picture of the Bethlehem star, supposedly marking the spot where Jesus was born, came a close second. Both were places where I felt I could pray and feel really close to the story of Jesus. I suppose that's what I mainly came for. We've had a lot of arguments and theological discussions about Jesus' life and his stories. Some of them I found difficult to follow, some of them I found a bit disturbing, especially when you indicated some things probably hadn't happened the way I always imagined them. And I sometimes wished I didn't have to hear such things. But it was probably good for me, and I certainly learnt a lot about Jesus and the Bible and the different ways the Gospels portray him.

So my view of Jesus has changed. I can see him now much more in first-century Palestine than in the green and pleasant land of the pictures of my first Bible! My understanding of the special names we give Jesus, like *Messiah* or *Son of God*, has deepened. And the whole idea of the kingdom of God has made me realize that the things we often argue about, whether we should be working more on the spiritual side or more on the social side, actually belong together. I'd like the people in church to understand that.

Having said all that, my fundamental understanding of the gospel, as being about God's love, hasn't changed. And seeing signs of love and faith at those holy sites was probably the most important and most inspiring thing for me.

Harold's page

I wanted to sign Brenda's page but Fiona wouldn't let me get away with it! I've obviously learnt a lot on this pilgrimage, especially since I haven't given religious matters much thought. There are lots of things I learnt about Jesus but I was particularly interested in the idea that he had these followers who literally followed him around and that that's where our expression of *following Jesus* comes from. I've always found it much easier to cope with Jesus than with church rituals. Brenda doesn't think I should say this, but they do make me feel uncomfortable.

Anyway, it was great to imagine Jesus in his homeland. In some ways, it made him more distant, in others more interesting. I suppose that is why I chose this picture of the Judaean wilderness – well, I just loved that desert landscape. And it's where I can imagine my favourite parable – the story of the Good Samaritan – to have taken place.

What I also remember especially well is what you had to say about miracles. Part of me felt it was chickening out to say they might not have happened like that, but part of me was also relieved that you looked at things rationally.

So thank you. I admit I got more out of this pilgrimage than I had expected.

Laura's page

I had a great time and I loved thinking and arguing with you, yes, and even worshipping with you! You know I'm particularly interested in contemporary political and social issues and I suppose my one fear before the pilgrimage was that we might get stuck in a religious heritage mould rather than concentrating on the present and the future. I was much enriched by learning more about Jesus' social context. I was particularly interested in the different parties who conspired in Jesus' death. I don't think I ever saw Jesus as a simplistic flower-power revolutionary figure, but it was good to discover more about what made him the person he was. I was particularly struck by the overlap between the religious and political significance of Jesus' life. So I place here a picture of the Church of St Peter Gallicantu – mainly because of the prison there which reminded us of political prisoners, intrigue and betrayal today. Easter is about overcoming death-dealing ways.

If you're asking for a practical outcome: The pilgrimage has fired me up to continue with my voluntary work in human rights.

Ian's page

I know I'm the one who could be a right pain to you and to some in the group for always raising historical questions. That's ultimately where it's at for me – but actually I think I also discovered that that isn't everything. Quite unexpectedly, I was often touched by our worship. There was at times a quality about it where time merged and past and future came together in God's presence which we called Jesus.

So I guess the main thing for me is that Jesus did not remain a figure in the past and therefore I might get more involved in the Church – though I shall remain interested in all those historical questions. I had to put a picture of the Qumran excavations here. Qumran fascinated me a long time ago and, when I heard it was on the itinerary, I knew I had to come.

Bill's page

I could not decide which picture to put here. At the beginning of the pilgrimage it would have been something to do with the crucifixion, by the end it had to be something of Easter. Though Jesus' crucifixion is still integral to my faith, I have come to see the resurrection as key to my faith in Jesus. So here's a picture of the Upper Room. When we talked about the Last Supper, I was very struck by how Jesus' life was primarily about God's kingdom and not about death. I was even touched by the announcement of Jesus' life in the annunciation story!

Of course, I learnt a lot about the Bible, even though I don't agree with some of the things you said, Julia. So I'm thinking of doing a study course on the Bible.

Richard's page

This is not an easy page for me to fill. You know there are lots of things I couldn't stomach in your teaching. I felt an outsider on the pilgrimage and was looking forward to being back home. But now I have questions gnawing away at me in my fellowship and I feel a bit homeless spiritually. In other words, the pilgrimage is certainly continuing for me, and I'm not sure where it's leading. Linda is disappointed that I'm not more positive and I don't dare tell her about all my doubts. I thought I knew who Jesus was when I came and hoped that the pilgrimage would build on that. Instead, I'm not sure what I'm left with now. Maybe I need to do some study, like Bill, but I don't know yet where I would go for that.

Perhaps my favourite memory is from the Mount of Beatitudes, see the picture. I was inspired then, at least for a moment, when I thought about Jesus living the beatitudes and Christians being called to follow him and live them as well.

Fiona's page

I'm a bit like the antipode to Ian. I came with no historic interest but realize now how much the historical dimension adds to our understanding. The day at Qumran was important for that.

My regret is that we did not engage more with particular faith communities in Israel-Palestine today, though I recognize you can't do everything. Having said that, I had a great time with you all and really enjoyed the variety of views in the group. That in itself was a good learning experience for me.

I also enjoyed the way I was able to glimpse the Jesus of the past through close attention to the biblical texts. It made him come very much alive for me.

You encourage a literary approach and I appreciate that. I especially remember our trip to Banyas, our discussions of the parables en route and thinking about the titles for Jesus when we got there.

So I attach a picture of the pools of water at Banyas, where you threw a stone in and likened the ripples to the effect of Jesus on the disciples and subsequent believers. Thank you, Julia.

Everyone clapped and thanked Fiona. Then it was over to Julia.

'Thank you very much for what each of you has contributed throughout the pilgrimage and by writing these pages. I've learnt quite a lot, too! Sharing with you all deepens my understanding of Jesus and strengthens my faith in his presence.

'Back here now, back in our communities, there's Jesus' work to be done. Thinking about our chat in the departure lounge, I suppose what is really important to me is that we don't think we're in Arrivals. With Jesus, we're always in Departures: he's ready for us at the gate, in for the long haul, as with all our questions and doubts we search for God's kingdom, proclaiming it and working for it.'

Questions for discussion

1. If you had been on this pilgrimage, which place would you have chosen to be pictured on 'your' page? Why?

2. What has the book done for you? (Think back to the first question at the end of Chapter 1.) Has your view of Jesus changed? Has anything else changed for you?

Notes

3 The River and the Desert

1. Mark 6.14–29; Matthew 14.1–12.
2. This prayer is taken from *Common Worship: Initiation Services*.
   Extracts from *Common Worship: Services and Prayers for the Church of England* are copyright © The Archbishops' Council 2000 and 2004.

4 Galilean Beginnings

1. From the Service 'Thanksgiving for Marriage' from *Common Worship: Pastoral Services*. Extracts from *Common Worship: Services and Prayers for the Church of England* are copyright © The Archbishops' Council 2000 and 2004.
2. From the hymn 'Dear Lord and Father of mankind' by J. G. Whittier.

6 The Sea of Galilee

1. Words by C. F. Alexander.
2. Common Worship Collect for St Andrew's Day. Extracts from *Common Worship: Services and Prayers for the Church of England* are copyright © The Archbishops' Council 2000 and 2004.

8 A Journey to Banyas

1. Luke 10.29–37.
2. Luke 15.11–32.

3. Matthew 20.1–16.
4. Matthew 25.31–46.
5. Mark 4.1–20; Matthew 13.1–23; Luke 8.4–15.
6. Mark 12.1–12; Matthew 21.33–44; Luke 20.9–19.
7. Mark 4.30–2; Matthew 13.31–2; Luke 13.18–19.
8. John 15.1–10.
9. Isaiah 5.
10. Luke 16.19–31.
11. See Daniel 7.13.

9 The Journey to Jerusalem

1. Luke 2.22ff.
2. Matthew 21.12–13.
3. John 2.13–22.
4. Zechariah 9.9.
5. Matthew 23.37–9.
6. Mark 13; Matthew 24; Luke 21.
7. Mark 11.11.
8. Luke 21.37.
9. Zechariah 14.4.
10. Mark 13; Matthew 24; Luke 21.
11. Prayer used by kind permission of Bishop Riah.

10 The Passion

1. From the hymn by Charles Wesley 'Lo, he comes with clouds descending'.
2. 1 Corinthians 11.23–5.
3. Mark 14.26–42.
4. Taken from *Book of A Thousand Prayers, The*, by Angela Ashwin. Copyright © 1996. Used by permission of The Zondervan Corporation.

5. John 19.5.
6. John 19.13.
7. Matthew 27.19.
8. Words by Richard Gillard © 1977 Scripture in Song (a division of Integrity Inc.) / Sovereign Music UK sovereignmusic@ aol.com.
9. Common Worship Collect for Good Friday. Extracts from *Common Worship: Services and Prayers for the Church of England* are copyright © The Archbishops' Council 2000 and 2004.

11 The Resurrection

1. Common Worship Ascension Day Collect. Extracts from *Common Worship: Services and Prayers for the Church of England* are copyright © The Archbishops' Council 2000 and 2004.
2. Common Worship Easter Day Collect. Extracts from *Common Worship: Services and Prayers for the Church of England* are copyright © The Archbishops' Council 2000 and 2004.

Suggestions for Further Reading

Bowker, John, *The Complete Bible Handbook: An Illustrated Companion*, 1998, Dorling Kindersley.

A reliable, beautifully produced source of information with an extensive section on Jesus and the Gospels.

Hamilton, William, *A Quest for the Post-Historical Jesus*, 1993, SCM Press.

A postmodern review of fictional treatments of Jesus.

Porter, J. R., *Jesus Christ: The Jesus of History, the Christ of Faith*, 1999, Duncan Baird.

A beautifully produced and illustrated book which can be read with benefit at various levels of depth.

Riches, J., *The World of Jesus: First-Century Judaism in Crisis: Understanding Jesus Today*, 1990, Cambridge University Press.

Excellent and accessible background reading.

Sanders, E. P., *Jesus and Judaism*, 1985, SCM Press.

One of the first and most influential Jesus books of the 'Third Quest'.

Theissen, G., *The Shadow of the Galilean: The Quest of the Historical Jesus in Narrative Form*, 1987, SCM Press.

The story of Jesus retold through the eyes of a Roman spy, with fascinating well-researched historical details.

Theissen, G. and Merz, A., *The Historical Jesus: A Comprehensive Guide*, 1998, SCM Press.

A truly comprehensive and scholarly guide, can be used as an encyclopaedia.

Theissen, G. and Winter, D., *The Quest for the Plausible Jesus: The Question of Criteria*, 2002, Westminster John Knox Press.

An academic book examining the criteria (and their theological and philosophical background) used in Jesus research and suggesting a new 'plausible' criterion.

Wright, N. T., *Christian Origins and the Question of God*, vol. 2: *Jesus and the Victory of God*, 1996, SPCK.

A foundational book in Bishop Tom Wright's series on Jesus.

Wright, N. T. and Borg, Marcus, *The Meaning of Jesus: Two Visions*, 1999, SPCK.

A great example of two renowned Jesus scholars engaging with each other's views on Jesus, looking at some of the most important controversial issues. Marcus Borg is a member of the 'Jesus Seminar'.